PRINCIPLES OF ANARCHO-CAPITALISM AND DEMARCHY

Antony P. Mueller

Antony P. Mueller

CONTENTS

Foreword

The policy agenda of the modern democracy asserts that government could prevent and cure unemployment, economic crises, recessions, depressions, inflation, deflation, and inequality and that the state could provide education, healthcare, and social security for all. The promises of rising incomes and employment dominate the political campaigns. Yet politics has never attained these assertions. In the time to come, the system of party politics will even less so fulfill its claims.

Yet the traditional policies have not worked, and they will even less so function in the new millennium. The answer is not more of the old, but that we must eliminate politics and the state. We have to do away with the conventional economic and social policies. Not more welfare state and government intervention are the answer but less state and more free capitalism.

The new technologies contain the solution of the problems they present. While technological progress destroys occupations, innovations make the economy more productive. Not growth and jobs are the key to the future but higher productivity.

New tools will make the political apparatus obsolete and allow to privatize the functions of government and of public administration. With the end of party politics and of the monopolistic state dominance, a colossal financial burden falls from the shoulders of the population. Imagine a world where the cost of living is only a fraction of today, and taxes and contributions require only a negligible part of income. With productivity so high that the purchasing power of the salaries would exceed that of today, the anxieties that afflict people nowadays about job security would dissipate.

In contrast to a system of free capitalism and of a stateless society, the contemporary social-democratic, 'liberal' system of governance marches on to more government spending, more public debt, and more regulation. The inner workings of the present system lead to higher taxes and more contributions. Public debt will continue to rise. The endpoint of the existing system of party democracy, social welfare, and state capitalism is not stability, wealth, and liberty but state bankruptcy, misery, and suppression. Without a change to a libertarian order of a stateless society, the road leads to a system where the new technologies will become the deadly instruments of comprehensive state control in the hands of a totalitarian regime.

In order to avoid a new totalitarianism, the answer is more capitalism and fewer politics. Such a libertarian order would do away with party politics through a system called 'demarchy' or 'sortition', which has the legislative body selected by lottery. A political system free of party politics together with introducing a market-based monetary order and the private provision of law and security would minimize and finally abolish the state as a monopolistic organization of dominance. An anarcho-capitalist order would open the way for the new technologies to do away with the avalanche of public policies and regulations and thus eliminate the present system, which is so inefficient, corrupt, unjust, and which is in its essence also undemocratic.

"Principle of Anarcho-Capitalism and Demarchy", highlights in the first part the exigencies of a political and economic order beyond the current system of state capitalism, political party politics, and government intervention. The second part discusses the structure of governance in a libertarian order and the details of a process of composition of the legislative body by random selection among the members of the constituency. The third part provides ten fundamental laws of economics as the guidelines of creating an anarcho-capitalist economic and political order. The booklet finishes with an outlook and is supplemented by extensive bibliographical references and an annotated bibliography of anarcho-capitalism by Hans-Hermann Hoppe as a basis for additional study and investigation.

INTRODUCTION

The State has become a burden on the economy. Contrary to the claims, economic policy does not promote stability and economic growth. Interventionism hampers productivity gains and weakens the fulcrum of prosperity.

No complex economy can prosper under the constraints of tribal moral rules. Guided by obsolete principles – such as social justice – the economy becomes fragile and less productive. Yet instead of changing the current economic system towards more capitalism, the reverse has been taking place. Capitalism has become more administrative. We are marching towards socialism, and the price we must pay for this error is growing.

The modern administrative state is active in all sectors of the economy and society. Money is in the hands of the state. As such, the state takes part in each monetary transaction. The public sector is present in the form of taxation, and government plays the role of an economic agent with spending, particularly in areas such as the military, health, pension, and education.

The interventionist state has taken hold of the economy. Yet the government's economic policies themselves provoke many of the evils that they allegedly heal. Instead of smoothing the economic cycle to stabilize the economy and to strengthen the factors that bring about economic growth, the impact of the monetary and fiscal policy weakens and destabilizes the economy. Economic policymakers ignore that fluctuations of the economic activities are natural and indispensable since they show to the entrepreneurs that there are distortions of the capital structure and that business management must, therefore, alter faulty allocations. Economic stimulus policies suppress the crisis signals. Yet these indications - such as the interest rate - are important to inform about how the economy runs and are necessary to incentivize companies to change inadequate projects in due course. When prices, wages, and interest rates do no longer serve as reliable economic indicators, the market mechanisms of adjustment become distorted and the economic operators continue to commit mistakes. Distortions spread throughout the economy and the longer and the more intensive the state intervention has worked, the more difficult it becomes to amend the production structure. The artificial boom which governments instigated, becomes the prelude to the next bust.

Guided by the false ideas that the media disseminate, and which form part of the syllabi at schools and universities, the government has become a suppressor of wealth creation.

It is time to abandon the myths about the state, politics and the economy. The modern political party system is neither democratic nor beneficial to the people. Parliaments are not representative of the people. The current international monetary system does not promote prosperity. To get out of these conundrums, more state and more politics will not help. We need a free society and a free economy. A decisive step to accomplish this goal is doing away with political elections. Modern technology allows the choice of representatives by random selection. A legislative Assembly whose members come into office by lot, even if larger than present parliaments, would cost less than an electoral system, be more representative, and in this sense would be much more democratic. With the length of service limited, the representatives would return to their civil life and their law-making would be free of the evils that come with the present political party system and its politicians whose main aim is the careerism.

***

Politics is an obstacle to wealth creation. Under the political system of the modern party-democracy, only a falsified kind of capitalism exists. The rule of the party democracy undermines the free market economy. In order to arrive at an unrestrained capitalism and to bring about an authentic market economy, there is a need to abolish politics. The less space there is for politics and the less there is government action, the faster a free capitalism will emerge. Such a change has become a necessity because we need an economic system of the highest productivity.

A step on the way to a free society would be, first, to establish a truly representative democracy by randomly selecting the people's delegates. Such an 'aleatory democracy', also called 'sortition', would set the conditions for a new legislation beyond the special interests that dominate a democracy based on elections. A body of randomly selected non-political law-makers would represent the people. Using public money to buy votes and to serve special interest groups to promote political careers would vanish. While the logic of the present system of political elections endorses government spending and more public debt and taxes, a randomly selected parliament would end the use of public money for buying votes. The role of the state would diminish along with the role of politics.

A further step toward free capitalism would be to end the central bank and to do away with the state monetary monopoly. A private monetary system would restrict the latitude of the state to spend. Doing away with a central bank and establishing a free money system would curtail the growth of public debt. The system of governance by political parties allows the deception according to which each citizen could live by the generosity of the state if only the right party would gain the election. A monetary system would unmask this fraud. Under free banking, the state loses its monopoly over the currency. The role of the national currency as the only 'legal tender' would disappear.

The libertarian revolution does not consist in a violent upheaval but comes through insight. Such a revolution requires an experimental approach. The victory of libertarianism does not requisite martyrs. A free capitalism will emerge as the economic system with the highest productivity when the shackles of the modern state will fall.

To some, the turning point to a true capitalism may seem utopian.

However, this objection has been valid for all political innovations. The ancient Greeks were talking about democracy, but they could not imagine a society without slavery. The Romans thought it impossible to rule without capital punishment. The monarchy was sacred to the people of the Middle Ages. Just as these beliefs of the past have vanished, today's political creeds that a society needs political parties, state money, state administration, and a public monopoly over the application of force to guarantee justice and security will also disappear.

I.

BEYOND THE STATE AND POLITICS

> *Finally, one can say it with certainty, the distrust of all rulers, the insight into the useless and wearisome nature of these short-lived struggles, must push people to a completely new conclusion: the abolition of the concept of the state, the abolition of the opposition 'private and public.' Step by step private companies take over the affairs of state: even the toughest remainder left over from the old work of government (the activity, for example, which is to secure the private against the private), will finally be provided by private entrepreneurs."*
> Friedrich Nietzsche: Human: All too human.
> Chapter 10. Item Eight "A Look at the State" (1878)

- *Economy and society –*
- *State capitalism –*
- *Backgrounder: the origins of modern state capitalism –*
- *Institutional change –*
- *Democracy and capitalism –*
- *Projects of transformation –*
- *At the crossroads –*
- *Outlook*

All existing political systems have their anchor in violence. This is also the case with democracy in a state that claims the monopoly over the use of force. Genuine capitalism, in contrast, requires a system of universal freedom and non-violence.

'Anarcho-capitalism' is the name of a governance that has property, freedom, and non-aggression as its first principles. In the political spectrum, libertarianism differs from the classical liberalism and is distinct from the American usage of the word 'liberalism'.

Classical liberalism put the property into the center of its system of governance. Yet the classical liberals were not strict enough in holding up the barrier against the erosion of the property rights. A political order of freedom requires a society with a minimum of state.

Freedom requires uncompromising adherence to the property rights and to voluntary exchange relations. As much market as possible - as little state as necessary refers only to the way. Ultimately, the ideal of anarcho-capitalism is to minimize and to abolish the state as the bearer of the monopoly of violence.

Yet anarchism in the sense of no authoritative force does not mean that order would not exist.

According to the ideal of the liberal order, there will be a legal and a social order in place - only that it will be private. Anarcho-capitalism demands private institutions that take care of internal and external security. Anarcho-capitalism does not promote anarchy but the transform of the state as a public institution into a private legal order.

Economy and Society

An economic order and society neither arise nor do they pass away independent of each other. The question is, which social system and which political order harmonizes best with a productive economic system. A free capitalism cannot develop within a political system dominated by violence. In the past, all political order grew out of violence and came from the systematic application of force. None of the existing systems of governance has produced a free capitalism. There has been no period in history when people could enjoy the full potential of a productive economic system.

Neither the French Revolution nor the American independence movement was peaceful. The Soviets took the government by force. Later, the Soviet Union instituted its vassal governments in Eastern Europe by force. West German democracy emerged from the ashes of the Second World War. The foundation of the Federal Republic of Germany took place as an occupied country under the weapons of the Allied armed forces. The Allies themselves had force as the source of their legitimacy because - be it the American, French, Russian or, as with England, the 'glorious' revolution – each one of these had violence as its springboard.

It has not been possible for a free society to assert itself since there have always been violent movements that have suppressed freedom. A libertarian economic and social order stands at the end of history. It is a seminal change because beginning with the formation of political communities, the motor of societal evolution has been violence. It was only step by step that violence has been brought under control and put aside by the economy as the driving force of development. Under anarcho-capitalism, this process would come to its fruition rejecting aggression in favor of the enthronement of voluntary economic exchange relations. Different from all other forms of governance, the legitimation of a libertarian order and its institutionalization comes from insight and not force.

Not the present 'liberal democracy' marks the end of history, but anarcho-capitalism means the end of the State.

In contrast to other political systems, anarcho-capitalism rests on the strict observance of the principle of non-aggression. Therefore, a libertarian system of governance cannot come into existence through force. In this sense, the libertarian social order stands at the end of the historical political development. It is the political system by default. Libertarianism marks the end of the political evolution after the alternatives have all failed.

The libertarian social order comes into being after it has become manifest that the previous political systems (democracy, monarchy, nobility, fascism, interventionism, communism, military dictatorship, etc.) have failed and will also fail in the future whatever their modifications.

Anarcho-capitalism works as a private contract society.

The principle of personal self-ownership means that all social rules must accord to this principle, and therefore no other instance is legitimate (including the so-called 'right' of the majority) to rule over the individual.

Private ownership determines the right of the individual to use his property, including the goods of production.

An anarcho-capitalist order requires the demise of the state and the de-politicization of society.

Foundational principles of anarcho-capitalism

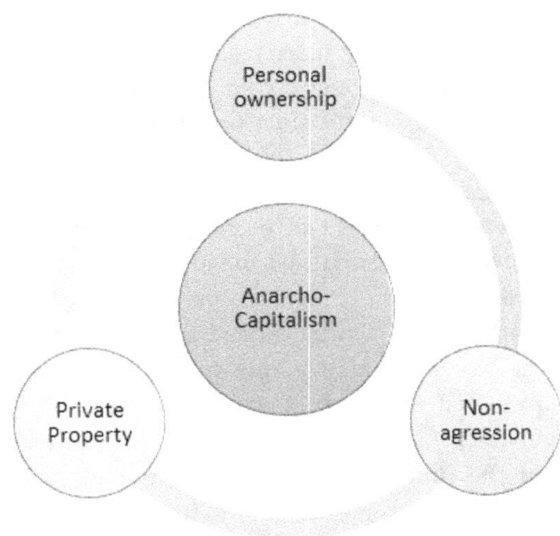

***

An anarcho-capitalist order becomes possible if the alternatives based on violence have lost their legitimacy. Libertarianism demands insight. No longer will be compulsion the way of political action, but political power itself will be subject to reason.

It is up to evolution whether the functions of the state continue as institutions, which are like the known state, and thus the state becomes smaller (the liberal order as a minimum state) - or if new forms of a state-free order will emerge. In principle, there can be free capitalism and a genuine 'rule of, by and for the people' only within an anarcho-capitalist order in which the monopoly of force of the state has disappeared and the political parties have vanished.

Antony P. Mueller

State Capitalism

In the political order of modern democracy, it is the majority vote with the principle 'one man, one vote', which distinguishes this system from the authoritarian forms of government of the earlier times. This political system, however, is a charade, because in democracy, too, the state apparatus prevails in an authoritarian and dictatorial manner. Democracy is not the rule of the majority but a tyranny of minorities. In the exercise of their tyranny, the democratic rulers, apparently legitimized by the majority vote, act as the proprietors of the state not much different from the manners of those who have come into power through violence, inheritance, tradition or charisma. The more the political parties and their leaders usurp the state, the less is the space for free capitalism. Not the people are in power in a democracy, but the leaders of the political parties and the representatives of special interest groups that direct the show behind the curtain.

The recent history of England – as the cradle of modern democracy – demonstrates how classical liberalism has failed. The liberalism of the nineteenth century has perished by the onslaught of party-democracy. As soon as the voting rights comprised persons without property, the days of the liberal order were over. However, England understood to delay this process of erosion. In the United Kingdom, during the 19th century, voting rights broadened to the less wealthy strata of the population. The rule 'one man – one voice' became valid after the third election reform of 1884, and until 1911, the Upper House, as the assembly of the Lords, could still veto the legislation of the Parliament (Lower House), while the suffrage of women in the United Kingdom began in 1928. So long as extending democracy to the masses was at bay, Great Britain flourished. The more the mass democracy took hold, the more the United Kingdom moved toward the slippery slope of economic decline. This fall was not because of the people. The broader the electorate became, the more prominent became party politics, and professional – mostly corrupt – politicians dominated the political game.

The economic systems that prevail in the world of today, even when called a 'market economy', is in the hands of a monopolistic state. In the modern state, there is no place for authentic capitalism and a true market economy. The economic systems of modern democracies are 'corporative capitalism' or 'state capitalism' with plutocratic and populist twists and turns.

Marxists call the present capitalism 'late' and designate the present time as 'post-capitalism' in contrast to the 'early capitalism' of the days of the industrial revolution. However, it is more appropriate to speak of the current system as 'pre-capitalism'. We are still at a stage before high capitalism, which is waiting to emerge.

Capitalist Evolution

After the early capitalism of the 19th century and the state capitalism of the 20th century, free capitalism is about to emerge in the 21st century.

Historical Stages of Capitalism

Early Capitalism (Take-off Capitalism)
- Mobilization of the factors of production capital and labor
- Savings and investment
- Capital accumulation
- Industrial Revolution
- Imperial expansion
- England
- 19th century

State Capitalism
- Systematic organization of production and distribution
- Discipline and control
- Strong link between state and the economy
- USA – Germany – Japan
- Economic nationalism
- 20th century

Full Capitalism
- Entrepreneurial innovation
- Connectivity and spontaneity
- Creative uncontrollability
- Separation of state and the economy
- Production clusters
- 'Digital cities'
- 21st century

***

Unlike state capitalism with its close interdependence between the state and the economy, entrepreneurial capitalism is independent of the state.

As a result, there is a de-politicization of society. Instead of nation and state, local – largely autonomous - production clusters are the centerpieces of the economy.

While capitalism of the nineteenth century aimed at mobilizing the factors of production and national capitalism, the hope for new millennium is that entrepreneurial capitalism will characterize the new epoch.

The creative uncontrollability of anarcho-capitalism will undermine the state's power in a natural way.

The capitalism of the nineteenth-century became global as imperialism and turned into the economic nationalism in the first part of the twentieth century to morph into the globalism of the nation-states in the second part of the 20th century. Now, '*glocalism*' (combining local and global) is emerging in the form of autonomous local units that are world-wide connected. The role of the nation-state makes way to *glocalization* and anarcho-capitalism. Like in the past, these great shifts do not happen without conflicts and setbacks.

'Glocalized anarcho-capitalism' is the socio-economic and political system of the future in contrast to the 'state capitalism' of the past.

Capitalist evolution

Take-off capitalism	Corporate state capitalism	Anarcho-capitalism
Mobilization of the factors of production	Efficiency of the organization of production and distribution	Innovation and entrepreneurship
Incentives to capital accumulation	Implementation of discipline and control	Laissez-faire of spontaneous order

***

The principle anarcho-capitalism asserts that the activities of the state are superfluous and harmful. It is true that the private sector cannot produce best results everywhere and all the time. Yet, the deficiencies of the private economy will not go away with state intervention. On the contrary. The belief that the state could do better than the market is the great illusion of our time. State intervention exacerbates the problems instead of solving them.

There are areas of production, which suffer from economic inefficiencies due to their special characteristics of demand and supply. Yet state intervention does not make supply more efficient nor does it solve the ethical conflicts.

The great illusion that the state could do away with social problems rests on a misconception of the nature of the human problems. Most economic and social problems do not have solutions but only trade-offs. Coping with these problems requires individual valuation and judgment. The state intervention does not resolve these problems but makes them worse. A collective cannot assess trade-offs. Only individuals can evaluate.

That the state still enjoys legitimacy, has three roots:

First, all non-libertarian systems came to power through force. The state as a repressive apparatus appears natural to most people. The uncoordinated and chaotic use of violence which is typical for conquering state-power gives way to the organized system of force under the state. This monopoly of violence of the state should protect against criminals within society, but in fact, it serves to control the behavior of all of its own citizens. The state does not stop with taxation but interferes with the private ways in many forms. Most people accept the authority and follow blindly. Only small groups liberate themselves from the state ideology. Constant propaganda about how necessary and important the state is keeps the thoughts and actions of most people captive in bondage.

Second, authoritarianism and dictatorship are as old as the state. Traditions continue to exist because any alternative does not come to mind as it is 'unthinkable'. Albeit many people recognize the absurdity of the rule of the state and the political madness that surrounds it, they perceive this insanity as normal, because they deem it unavoidable.

Third, special interests mark day-to-day politics and the election process. Many voters are victims of the political propaganda and confound their own interests with the privileges of other groups.

Few people recognize that there is an alternative to state capitalism, democracy, communism, socialism, fascism, and the modern welfare-warfare state. Libertarianism as a new enlightenment changes the public opinion so that the infantile attitude to turn to the state as the universal problem solver will end. Getting rid of politics and the state must disavow the naïve attitude, which assumes as a principle without further ado, that the state can and should and must act as a problem-solver when in fact politics and the state are major sources of our troubles.

Backgrounder:
The origins of the modern state capitalism

State capitalism is a regime where the state exerts direct control over a large part of the economy. It is the preferred system of authoritarian and dictatorial regimes because it facilitates to keep the ruler in power. Yet state capitalism is also compatible with the oligarchical political system of party democracy.

Whatever was left of liberal capitalism vanished in the ashes of World War I in the years from 1914 on. The war economy became the great inspiration for central planning and government control of the economy. In as much as World War I was the womb to give birth to Soviet Communism and Nazism, it is also the cradle of the interventionist welfare-warfare state. In the 20th century, state capitalism with its multitude of variants has become the dominant socio-economic and political system. This system is now in crisis.

The principle of state capitalism is bribery; it is a system which bribes itself to power and keeps itself at the power through corruption. The beneficiaries of corruption range from corporations to trade unions and to the general bureaucracy and to specific state sectors such as the military or the education establishment. State capitalism expands as the welfare-warfare state whereby one or the other tendency may preponderate. Among the varieties of state capitalism, there is the authoritarian and the populist variant, the welfare type and the warfare type, the plutocratic, corporatist and kleptocratic variants and the respective number of combinations.

The American state capitalism concentrates on warfare, welfare, and corporatism, for example, while Switzerland is plutocratic but not biased towards warfare. State capitalism is organized in 'complexes', such as the 'industrial-military complex', the 'pharmaceutical-health complex' and the 'research and higher education complex' among others such as, for Germany, for example, the 'automobile industry complex'.

What differentiates the countries in their economic performance is the degree to which they are competitive or protectionist. Countries such as Denmark and Switzerland share with the US a competitive and open economic system different from Brazil, for example. Brazil has a kleptocratic state capitalism that lacks a competitive economic system and favors protectionism, which moves it closer to Russia or Nigeria in terms of economic performance.

Because it is based on bribery, the system of state capitalism is in permanent financial need. State authorities are desperate to promote economic growth and employment as the sources of state power. Tax receipts are never large enough to finance all the desired public spending. Modern state capitalism must resort to debt financing, which, in turn, makes this system biased towards inflation. State capitalism cannot survive. The great topic of the 21st century will be which socio-economic and political system should replace state capitalism. It is not capitalism that is in crisis, but it is state capitalism that is moribund. In as much as state capitalism has become the dominant system of governance during the past one hundred years, the death struggle of state capitalism marks the great battle of transition to the new libertarian system of free capitalism.

The pivotal event to launch modern state capitalism was World War I. This conflict experienced mass conscription and an outbreak of national fanaticism. It created the 'war is the health of the state' syndrome. World War I was the launching pad for Fascism, Communism, National Socialism, state interventionism, and all other kinds of ideological totalitarianism. World War I and II eliminated the difference between the military and the civil population when governments promoted the total war with the state as the organizer of genocide and democide.

The organizational root of state capitalism is fascism. The "Fascist Manifesto" proclaimed in 1919 by Alceste De Ambris and Filippo Tommaso Marienetti demanded universal suffrage and proportional regional representation of the electorate. The authors called for establishing a corporatist system of 'National Councils' formed by experts who were to be elected by their professional organizations and who should hold legislative power in their respective areas. The Manifesto called for an eight-hour work day and a minimum wage; it demanded worker representation in industrial management and equal standing of trade unions, industrial executives, and public servants. The authors of the Fascist Manifesto called for progressive taxation, invalidity insurance, and other types of social insurance, along with reducing the retirement age, the confiscation of the property of all religious institutions, and nationalizing the armament industry.

The Fascist Program
according to the Fascist Manifesto of 1919
("Il manifesto dei fasci di combattimento")

We demand:

a) Universal suffrage polled on a regional basis, with proportional representation and voting and electoral office eligibility for women.

b) A minimum age for the voting electorate of 18 years; that for the office holders at 25 years.

c) The abolition of the Senate.

d) The convocation of a National Assembly for a three-years duration, for which its primary responsibility will be to form a constitution of the State.

e) The formation of a National Council of experts for labor, for industry, for transportation, for the public health, for communications, etc. Selections to be made from the collective professionals or of tradesmen with legislative powers and elected directly to a General Commission with ministerial powers.

For the social problems: We demand:

a) The quick enactment of a law of the State that sanctions an eight-hour workday for all workers.

b) A minimum wage.

c) The participation of workers' representatives in the functions of industry commissions.

d) To show the same confidence in the labor unions (that prove to be technically and morally worthy) as is given to industry executives or public servants.

e) The rapid and complete systemization of the railways and of all the transport industries.

f) A necessary modification of the insurance laws to invalidate the minimum retirement age; we propose to lower it from 65 to 55 years of age.

For the military problem: We demand:

a) The institution of a national militia with a short period of service for training and exclusively defensive responsibilities.

b) The nationalization of all the arms and explosives factories.

c) A national policy intended to peacefully further the Italian national culture in the world.

For the financial problem: We demand:

a) A strong progressive tax on capital that will truly expropriate a portion of all wealth.

b) The seizure of all the possessions of the religious congregations and the abolition of all the bishoprics, which constitute an enormous liability on the Nation and on the privileges of the poor.

c) The revision of all military contracts and the seizure of 85 percent of the profits therein.

Source: Conservapedia

✳✳✳

Since its inception, fascism was the main rival of communism with the question open which creed offered the better or rather the worse kind of socialism.

In 1922, Benito Mussolini came to power in Italy and put into practice most of the fascist program that he proclaimed. Adolf Hitler came into government in Germany in 1933 and installed a more radical version of the fascist program which included also a genocidal agenda. In the developing world, Brazilian President Getúlio Vargas (President from 1930 to 1945 and from 1951 to 1954) was inspired by both Mussolini and Hitler and introduced a vast arrangement of protective labor laws which gained him the support of the labor unions and the working class. Vargas established the Brazilian version of fascism. Argentina adopted a kind of personalized fascism in the form of Peronism after World War II. Juan Domingo Peron became president in 1946 and set Argentina on the path of what can be called 'populist fascism'. General Francisco Franco established a fascist state in Spain in 1939 after winning the civil war (1936-1939), and Antônio de Oliveira Salazar established an authoritarian regime with strong fascist tendencies in 1933. Japan established a fascist regime in 1931, and China under Chiang Kai-shek in 1932.

By the early 1930s, fascism had become a global movement. Hitler succeeded with his economic program in doing away with mass unemployment. While the depression ravaged on in the United States, unemployment fell in half by 1935 in Germany and the country approached full employment by 1936, the year when John Maynard Keynes published his theory on how to overcome depressions. Government programs to stimulate the economy was the trademark of the Hitler regime. All he had to do for that purpose was to implement the plans in the drawers of the state bureaucracy of the governments before him. These plans were not put into practice because of the depression. Hitler's ploy was to launch the government programs combined with price and wage controls. This way the inflationary consequences of Hitler's economic policy remained hidden. In the United States, state capitalism experienced a heyday when president Richard Nixon implemented price and wage controls in 1971. This time, the policy's name was 'incomes policy' and received its blessing from Keynesian economic theory

Compared to the times of relative laissez-faire during the 19th century, the 20th century up to the present has been the era of national-socialism and international socialism and its manifold variations.

Modern state capitalism received its characteristic shape and contents in its fascist period. One might even say fascism has never ended but instead transmogrified into its present subtle forms. Yet in terms of its interventionist, anti-liberal character, modern state capitalism is not much different from its predecessor. In the modern state capitalism, the social claims of fascism are obvious although its nationalist and xenophobic strains were tamed and re-channeled into less deadly endeavors, such as international sports events.

After World War II, an expanding state capitalism has gone hand in hand with the spread of social democracy, which has become the dominant political ideology of the modern state. Social democracy or what is called 'liberalism' in America, is the soft mixture of both Communism and fascism. Almost each major political party, even if they do not have 'social' or 'democratic' in their name, profess the values of social democracy. Social democracy (or 'liberalism' as in the United States) is the unifying band across the mainstream political parties. It makes often only a minor difference whether the more 'right' or the more 'left' party forms the government.

In hindsight, fascism and Communism appear as the radical variants of the social democratic mainstream. It is, therefore, no surprise that both extremes still lurk behind the veil of tamed social liberalism - always ready to move into prominence.

Once it became accepted that the *raison d'être* of 'the state' would be to provide 'social justice' and 'social security', the classical liberal notion that government activity has limits had to make room for unbound state activity because different from hunger and shelter, for example, 'social justice' does not have a natural saturation point. While in the 19th century, it was the defense of liberty that served as the norm to limit state activity, this criterion has disappeared in favor of comprehensive 'rights'.

The 20th century experienced the rise of the social democracy as that political movement whose major plank is the claim of distributional rights, such as the right to work, the right to holidays, the right to social security, the right to free education, and so on with the expanding social rights agenda for so-called minorities. Equality is the battle cry of this movement.

Major steps in the project to establish the interventionist welfare state and state capitalism came with the rise of international organizations after World War II such as the United Nations, the International Monetary Fund, and the World Bank. Regional advances were made by creating the European Economic Community in 1957 and launching a common European currency in 1999. The warfare side of post-war state capitalism experienced a major advance with NATO and the Warsaw Pact during the Cold War. By these steps, state capitalism has become international and more efficient – both in its military and economic prowess. In as much as capitalism has become more productive after the end of World War II, national and global institutions have grown to control capitalism and shape it in a way that optimizes its capacity to serve as a host for the parasitic state activity.

Yet one cannot ignore the signs that the social democratic age including its two radical manifestations of fascism and communism is ending. Free capitalism and a libertarian political order now is the natural way to go. It is only due to tradition and lack of imagination that holds the people back. Rather than moving forward to the new system, some groups even favor one or the other of the radical variants of social democracy although no one with a sane mind could be in favor of either fascism or communism.

Institutional Change

The course of history follows not a pre-determined path but depends on the decisions we make. However, the presence is connected with the past because the current circumstances are the result of past decisions and events. The past is gone yet relevant insofar as it has determined our present situation. Beyond that, we must take new decisions at every moment. While the presence results from the past, the future is the effect of our present decisions. That the presence follows from past does not mean that the past determines the decisions we shall take today. This also holds for political institutions.

It is true that the current situation is the outcome of what has been decided before under the circumstances that then prevailed. While, of course, one cannot change the past, it is not so that the past would determine the future. Although we are free to choose institutions, we are not free from the consequences that follow from our decisions. Because history could have been different as it was, so our present situation and our future can be different as well.

In politics and society, there is freedom to choose specific institutions, yet each decision has its proper consequences. Each institution unfolds its own dynamics. A society may be free what institution it chooses but once an institution is in place, it becomes 'a fact' in social life. Institutions differ from 'culture'. What distinguishes North Korea from South Korea is not its culture but the institutions in North and South Korea.

No individual and no society are bound by 'culture' or 'tradition' but only by the belief in culture or tradition.

Each state constitutes itself as a monopolistic enterprise to apply force. The state as such, as we know it, suffers from the evils that come with a single provider. A monopoly, be it a private company or the state, is inefficient, resistant to innovation, and released from constraints to care for its customers. With the state, it is worse because the state has the monopoly of violence. The state, as the holder of the 'legitimate' physical force, is an attraction to psychopaths of all kind and to all those who seek power to satisfy their craving for dominance over other people's lives. What is political history but the story how bizarre men and women have conquered and abused their powers?

State supremacy, which exists as a monopoly in domestic politics, also drives their holders to extend their sphere of dominance to other countries. Throughout history, peaceful times and good rulers have been only short breaks in an ongoing tragedy, in which one wretched creature after the other at first tries to dictate over his countrymen and then strives to rule the world. The 'grip on the world power' comes to every political leader. Only resistance from other groups can keep these power-hungry madmen at bay. If this resistance fails, the monopolistic state goes berserk. With the state apparatus at his hand, the leader receives the arsenal of the public propaganda tools. The ruler of a country can manipulate the popular opinion and incite one nation to go to war against another without rational cause. International politics exceeds the madness of domestic politics.

The theorists who study parliamentary democracy say that the competition among political parties and the division of powers could keep state violence in check and hold its abuse under control. Yet there is abundant evidence that modern democracy offers no solution to the conundrum of the monopoly of the power of the state.

One can imagine how a free social order will work. With all the other systems of governance, it is the opposite. These ideologues do not know how their plans will work in reality but they are keen to install it anyhow. The Communists, for example, did not know how socialism could ever function, but they were resolute in their desire to get there - and be it by brutal force. The difficult task for the libertarians is to find out how to establish a non-aggression order when force is out of the question. The anarcho-capitalist worldview differs from the other political ideologies that the libertarians follow the principle non-aggression.

Different from libertarianism, the radical parties of the right or the left and even those of the center, can always opt for violence to establish and preserve their favored order. While the non-libertarian political movements want to seize power to exercise it, anarcho-capitalism wants to minimize the role of force and supremacy in society.

Antony P. Mueller

Democracy and Capitalism

The political election campaigns in the popular democracies consist in a competition among political parties about which party will promise the best to specific groups. An election in a democracy is about slogans and half-truths. There is a competition between parties, but the persons who represent these parties form a kind of band of their own. The modern politicians are apart from the people - not much different as it once was the case with the aristocracy. This separation comes with the use of force. The authority over violence sets the rulers apart from the ordinary people.

Modern democracy suffers from the contradiction that while most citizens mistrust the politicians and the state, and want fewer taxes and less state control, each voter is eager to use his vote in such a way as to get the largest piece of the cake. Such a system is neither democratic nor capitalist; it is corrupt as it produces a political game in which each voter tries to cheat all the other voters. The principle of modern democracy is that while the voters try to cheat one another in getting a free lunch, the political establishment cheats all of the voters.

The dominant system in the industrialized countries of today is neither capitalist nor democratic but the rule is 'state capitalism'. It has surfaced in the beginning of the 20th century and over the century it has transformed from authoritarian to democratic fascism. No longer prevails an authoritarian one-party system but in the modern democracy, people are in power who form a network which, although they take part in a competitive game with each other, do so together as a group. This democracy operates like a one-party system with various factions.

The results of an election about who forms the government gets decided at the margin, which means the great bulk of the leading members of the party that lost an election will not leave politics but stay on as the opposition and continue in the power play. Different from a bankrupt company which vanishes from the market, in politics, the losers of an election remain in the game and continue their activity – be it as members of the opposition or as coalition partners for the party that has 'won' the elections. Other than their role in the game, nothing has changed.

Under the conditions of the ruling fiduciary monetary system and the existing majority voting right, the current system does not move towards a free market economy even if most people should want so. Instead of an anarcho-capitalist order, there is a tendency to an interplay between left- and right-wing populism, between short pauses of peace and the return of terror and violence. In this sense, all modern parties in a democracy are social-fascist parties and the modern state is a democratic social- fascist state.

Libertarianism in the political spectrum

The political left, as well as the political right, recognize the authoritarian state power. In contrast to libertarianism, personal freedom of the individual is not their focus on the political value scale, but the state.

While 'The Left' refers to 'society' for legitimacy, 'The Right' reclaims as their legitimation basis 'the nation'.

The position of libertarianism in the political spectrum

"The Left"	Libertarianism	"The Right"
• Authoritarian state power • Society • Universal welfare state • International socialism	• Personal liberty • Individual • Economic freedom • Decentralization	• Auhoritarian state power • Nation • National welfare state • National socialism

In contrast to these two positions, the individual is at the center of political values for fundamental liberalism.

The leftist movements strive for a universal welfare state while right-wing political parties advocate a social state of a national character.

Libertarianism, in contrast, rests on economic freedom.

International socialism is the ultimate organizational aim of the left while the right is striving for National Socialism.

The political organizational ideal of libertarianism is the city-state or the regional minority, in contrast to the national greatness of the right and the internationalism of the left.

In order to arrive at a libertarian governance without violence, public opinion must change. Libertarianism has to offer visions and models to explain what is going on and can transform the public opinion in favor of a libertarian future. For this purpose, radical anarchist models are inappropriate. It is necessary to convince the public about the practical feasibility of libertarianism and to show that anarcho-capitalism is not only a theory, but practical and just. Beyond that one cannot and must not plan the transition to libertarianism. Its institutions must come about as a spontaneous order. A libertarian order is conceivable, and one can describe and explain how it does work, but the way to its realization must be evolutionary and spontaneous. Different from other political concepts, public opinion must not follow the lead, but for libertarianism, public opinion itself must be the leadership. Not violence and grand plans provide the path to a libertarian order, but a series of practical steps that provide the basis for a free society to unfold.

Projects of Transformation

Not for their establishment, but for their preservation, the political system needs the approval of public opinion. Power never exists as a crude force alone. State power dominates and falls with its legitimacy, which comes from the approval of public opinion. The great dictatorships of the twentieth century received their position of power from the belief in certain ideologies. Not the brutal violence made their rule possible, but the consent of the masses allowed the governments to use brutal force. Today, the belief in democracy as majority rule dominates the mindset of the population and forms the basis of legitimacy of this system. Yet democracy in the form of the majority voting system leads to interventionism, and from there, socialism is only a step away. Democracy does not protect against folly or tyranny.

How can one redesign the political system towards more freedom? In the first step, one must deprive the existing system of 'liberal' democracy of its false legitimacy and to show the alternative.

A false legitimation relates, first, to money. Habit and lack of knowledge are the reasons that for many people there is no alternative to the present system although there is a lot of uneasiness with the monetary order. In the modern economy, the state has the monopoly over money. Yet why this is so, there is no rational answer. With the national central bank, the state has a central command body over the financial system. This monetary system rests on centralism and monopolism. Central banking stands in opposition to the free capitalism.

The members of the central bank are among the most important holders of power. They come into these positions on intricate and opaque paths. Like the Constitutional Court, the members of the Central Bank are appointed. In the same way, as the supreme judges act as masters of the Constitution by pretending to protect them, the members of the central bank are the masters of the money system and claim to preserve the value of money. Not different from the 'protectors of the Constitution' as masters of constitutional transformation, the central bankers – as proclaimed 'guardians of our currency' – are the main culprits of the monetary havoc and the financial crises that have afflicted capitalism. In monetary matters, central bankers rule over the economy like a Soviet central committee. How these members of the uppermost power elite come into the respective positions remains hidden, and what they do is frightening.

The failure of the central bankers is no less apparent than the problem with the disgraceful verdicts of the supreme judges. The central bankers are responsible for the big economic catastrophes of the twentieth century: the hyperinflation of the 1920s in Germany and the Great Depression of the 1930s in the USA. The stagflation of the seventies is the produce of the mismanagement of central bankers as well as the financial crisis of 2008. Over the next ten years, the combined efforts of the central banks of the US, Japan, and Europe have instigated the largest speculative bubble the world has ever seen. By implanting interest rates that are below any reasonable level, central bankers have fueled a global speculative frenzy of gigantic proportions. Nevertheless, the media put the blame on 'capitalism', and praise central bankers and finance minister as the 'saviors' of the system. The public gets deceived by the pundits in academia and the media who praise the wolves as the guardians of the sheep.

The task is to reform the monetary system and to curb the national debt and to get to a real democracy. The existing monetary regime is a state–political instrument for the exercise of power, which allows the unrestrained expansion of the welfare state, war–making, and to accumulate public debt. A new monetary order is a decisive step towards the new economic order. The change of the system can come within the framework of the prevalent legal basis. Abolishing the state monopoly on money and to recognize private money as a means of payment is the way to start the reform of the monetary system. The point is to give back to the citizens the freedom of monetary choice over which currency to use. Economic actors should be free to decide which money they would like to have for their transactions.

As a first step, one must eliminate the prime position of the central bank as a central planning body. This can be done by imposing a limit on the quantity of the central bank money. If the central bank no longer has access to manipulating the money supply, it can no more manipulate the basic rate of interest. After that, it should be easy to phase out the central bank as a public institution by sending the officeholders into retirement. This measure would eliminate the main source of cyclical turmoil. Freezing the quantity of central bank money will put a brake on the government to accumulate debt and thus also help to neutralize the role of governmental interventionism as the other main source of creating economic havoc besides central banking.

***

As a second step, the plan comes into play of reforming the electoral system and to do away with the political class. Ending the current electoral system of majority vote in favor a a lottery for selecting the representatives of the people, would eliminate party politics and the professional politicians. With the modern means of communication, it is possible to select a representative body of the population by random sampling. According to this model of the political lottery, the members of this group would form the Legislative Assembly. Such an Assembly would be participatory and representative. Selecting the people's representative by lot would be also cheaper than the election campaigns and to maintain parliaments and congresses in their present forms. This Assembly would then hire private government management companies - to exert the function of government under the strict supervision of the Assembly.

In the United States, the Freedom Movement could push for this election model in individual states and from there the movement could spread across the country until after a phase of experimentation it could serve for the election of the members of Congress. In Europe, one could start with the city councils of the metropolitan areas. As a transitory method, one could also consider forming a kind of 'Upper House' or 'Senate' by the random selection of its members. This House would oversee the actions of the members of Congress and be the ultimate body of the approval of the laws. This assembly should have full veto power over new laws. The assembly would be composed of members who are selected by a rolling lottery with each member serving for two years has many advantages over the present system.

Private government management companies would emerge on competitive markets and offer their services first at the municipal and the state level and from there comprise larger entities up to the level of a country or a union of states. Private government management companies would be in the business to earn a profit and as such they must satisfy the demands of their client (which is the people represented by the Assembly) at the lowest cost.

Such a system would lead to the following consequences (for more detail see the last chapter on 'anarcho-capitalism':

First, serious policymaking in favor of the best for the population would replace the current political game plays that serves special interest groups.

Second, the random selection system would bring a wide range of expertise to the political system.

Third, the members of such an Assembly would not be power-hungry psychopaths and political careerists because, after their short period of life in politics, these persons would return to their private life.

Finally, such legislative procedures would give priority to cut government spending and to lower the tax burden because the members of the Assembly will be the ones who must pay for them.

One may expect that with 'demarchy', government spending will fall, taxes will be lower, and bureaucracy will be less.

The third project treats the legal and the security system. At present, the judicial order is contradictory since the judiciary itself is part of the political system about which it decides. To speak of the 'independence' of the courts is as unrealistic as to claim that the central banks are independent. The state-jurists praise the division of power, yet their existence proves otherwise and underlines that to realize the principle is impossible and exists only as a myth.

De-politicization, de-bureaucratization, and the private organization of justice, as well as internal and external security, are the mainstays on the way to establish a libertarian economic and social order.

Doing away with the professional politician, and of party politics, comes with the electoral reform that stipulates the selection of the legislative assembly by the principle of chance.

***

Main steps to an anarcho-capitalist order

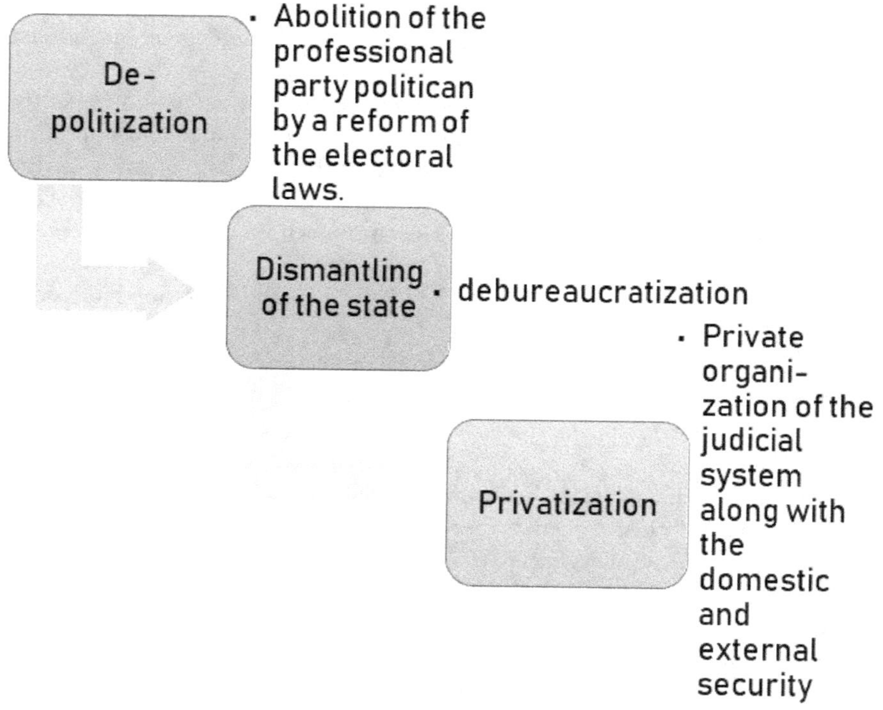

***

The legislative body will promote the de-bureaucratization of the state. Finally, the private organization of justice and internal and external security comes into existence.

In the modern political state, the division of powers is a fallacy, for the political parties are not only present in the legislative body but are also in government as well as they appoint the judges, including the members of the

32

Constitutional Court. A state legal system is not independent as it exists in close ties to the prevailing power structure. All moral aberrations of the Zeitgeist sneak into the jurisprudence: from the local jurisdiction to the constitutional courts. There has been no perversity on this earth which was not legal at scme time and with which the courts did not collaborate.

Not only the United States suffers from the discrepancy between the value system prevalent at the courts and that of the population. The loss of trust in the law has become as severe as the loss of confidence in politics.

A private system of jurisprudence would end with the exercise of the authority of the public judiciary over the people. A private legal system would cost less, be more effective and it would be more just. Artificial intelligence would come to its full potential under a private legal system and cut expenses for legal services to a small fraction of what it costs now.

At the Crossroads

Populist interventionism is the most widespread economic system. The countries differ by whether they are more active or less active in interventionism. Money is under the control of the state. The state mingles in the economic transactions through taxation. While some sectors are more under state control than others, the visible consequence is that these sectors where crises persist – such as the internal and external security, healthcare, old-age provision, education, money, and finance – are those, which are under the most intensive governmental control. A huge apparatus of subsidies sustains at huge costs the defense industry, the automobile sector, pharmaceuticals companies, large parts of the agricultural, and educational institutions.

***

Although the great debate no longer takes on the alternative between socialism and capitalism, the central question remains: whether society should move more to state intervention or more to a market economy. This way, the traditional question of socialism or capitalism is still on the table.

History does not have an inevitable path of development, but there are economic laws. The decision for this or that version of the economic system is free, but the consequences are not free to choose. Freedom refers to the choice of institutions, not to their consequences.

In this sense, there is a power of ideas, and at the same time, there is the impotence of ideas in the face of facts. There are situations where, as they say, that one cannot change the things anymore. Before one made the wrong decision, the options were open as they laid on the table. A different choice could have avoided the problems that have surfaced now as consequence of the wrong decision and the course of history would have gone in another direction.

As in the 1930s, socialist ideas can conquer the United States again as they did get hold of Europe since the beginning the 20th century.

There is a tendency to choose socialism without considering what consequences will come with this choice. Emotions and prejudices are behind why socialism remains attractive. Despite its evocations of science, socialism is a fairy-tale for adults. Following their creed, the socialists dream of a society where righteousness and prosperity rule together with equality of all.

The infantile socialization of the upbringing reinforces the biological disposition for socialism because children and adolescents live under the socialist systems of the family, the schools, and the university until they are grown-up and often remain under the socialist spell for the rest of their lives.

It is through the efforts of the reason it becomes possible to free oneself from the socialist faith. The first step to deliverance from the socialist creed is the insight that not redistribution helps the poor, but rather economic growth and a free capitalism, which increases productivity and income.

Ironically, it was the success of capitalism that created the socialist expectation of a world without scarcity. The capitalist experience showed that a prosperous world was no longer a utopian fantasy.

The early socialists were convinced that socialism would increase the productivity of capitalism not despite but because of the equality of distribution. In the socialist paradise, one could have a greater material abundance than under capitalism along with the eradication of all kinds of injustices and discriminations. Socialism arises from the desire for the kingdom of Cockaigne. The driving motif of the early socialist movement was idealism. Today, this utopian system promises to the gullible that the smartphone comes free of charge, along with a free public transportation system and the purchase of a generous citizen's pension, as well as, of course, a guaranteed minimum income and free education and healthcare of the highest standards for all.

Some in the socialist movements find their way to socialism out of a personal need for social justice or based on religious motives. Among the wealthy and the rich heirs, there are socialists because of a bad conscience about their wealth. Yet the dream of a fair distribution is a great illusion.

First, the amount to distribute would be less than many socialists believe. For example, if the billionaires in the Forbes list would share all their wealth with the rest of the world's population, every single person on earth would receive no more than the single payment of an amount of the size of a moderate monthly salary of the workmen in the rich countries.

Second, even if the current billionaires would agree to this plan, they could not do so because their wealth does not consist in money but in shares and other business interests and in real estate. To distribute the money, the owners would have to sell these assets. Yet if they sell, who will buy?

Third, if one should want to apply a more drastic measure in the name of social justice and one would distribute by force the wealth of the world equally, it would take a short time, and a new uneven distribution would soon come back into existence, with the additional consequence that the overall poverty in the world would have become greater in the process.

If the redistribution in capitalism does not work, so some seem to ponder, only to impose full socialism will solve the problem of 'injustice'. In doing so, these socialists believe that they are good-hearted when they advocate socialism, yet they do not know that they speak in favor of an inhuman regime whose first victims by all probability would be themselves.

The great ideological battle continues in waves, although millions of people fell victim when the socialist terror regimes dominated the conflicts of the 20th century. History has shown that socialism in its international Soviet variant and in its national-socialist form can only exist through as tyranny. With the decision for interventionism and socialism, economic stagnation comes with this choice. In contrast, with the decision for a free market economy, the choice leads to economic progress. Theories and history show that socialism brings a compulsory economy and leads to stagnation, suppression, and poverty while capitalism is more productive the freer it is.

The 21st century will belong to those nations that choose the path to free capitalism while those countries that opt for socialism and interventionism will suffer economic stagnation and decline.

The alternatives are clear. On the one hand, free capitalism as an economic order that brings with it personal liberty and overall prosperity, and, on the other hand, the socialist command economy, leading to poverty and imprisonment.

A look at the experiences with the Communist rule in Eastern Europe and Asia and in other parts of the world makes the diagnosis unambiguous. Yet, instigated by insistent propaganda, popular discontent runs against the capitalist economic order. The media create the illusion that one could have both the wealth of capitalism and the supposed socialist equality and justice.

Socialism of the twentieth century is no longer the dominant ideology of our time, but anti-capitalism is still virulent, and this ideology is all over in the media, the schools, and the universities. The great error of the socialist is to believe that that poverty originates from capitalism and not from the interventionism that they themselves preach and practice. It should be obvious to everyone that socialism in all its variants is not a solution but a highway to hell. Communism has abdicated, but it has impregnated a powerful backstage in the form of poisonous anti-capitalism. Socialist desires are still virulent. It is dormant in many heads and often benign in its present forms, yet the socialist monster and Communist suppression can rise again at any moment.

This time, the regimes of terror would have a gigantic arsenal of modern technology at their disposal. Future dictatorships would be able to cement their power in a degree which was unheard of from the past. In this sense, the option for anarcho-capitalism is a choice for life over death.

Outlook

It would be a misunderstanding to characterize the libertarian order as 'anarchistic' in the sense of chaos and disorder. On the contrary. Anarcho-capitalism is the opposite of anarchy, mayhem, and lawlessness. Anarchy, chaos, and disorder characterize the present system. Free capitalism carries the social order within itself, as a system of governance that is free from the state. The road to a libertarian order is a revolution that is not disruptive. Libertarianism is an evolutionary system, not one that could or should be imposed from above or from the outside.

The vision and the models of an anarcho-capitalist order are clear. What is necessary for this transformation to succeed is a majority for an electoral reform, which would introduce the random selection principle of representatives. After the accomplishment and benefits of the anarcho-capitalist order become visible, libertarianism would spread by imitation. It takes only a few communities to adopt the principles of anarcho-capitalism and over time the libertarian order would find followers in other communities and countries.

We are at a crossroads. Like the decades of before and after 1800, when the industrial revolution took off, those nations that did not recognize the signs of the time fell behind. The countries, which delayed or missed the industrialization, have suffered the loss of prosperity until our present days. Today, the world faces a similar challenge. Again, we must choose and take a decision. This time it is about more or less capitalism. Less capitalism will lead to socialism - whether or not one would want it - and thus to the misery associated with such a regime. The right way for the 21st century is the choice in favor of free capitalism. The future belongs to those countries that choose capitalism free from the state and from politics as their system of governance.

The triumph of real capitalism entails self-liberation according to which the individual finds himself, becomes his own, and delivers himself from the false dependencies and deceptive duties. Such a new order can only arise through voluntary action from which it derives its legitimation.

II.

ANARCHO-CAPITALISM

*"Gentlemen, the time is coming when there
will be two great classes, Socialists, and Anarchists.
The Anarchists want the government to be nothing,
and the Socialists want government to be
everything."*
William Graham Sumner (1911)

- The State and its minions
- Voluntary servitude
- The age of the individual
- What is anarchism?
- Concepts
- Is Anarcho-capitalism possible?
- The struggle for liberty
- Death of the gatekeepers
- Toward the new world of freedom
- Sortition (demarchy)
- Agenda
- Outlook

The process of substituting labor through machines enters sectors that have seemed to be exempt from automatization and robotization. The new technologies will transform law, medicine, education, consulting, business administration, and the public service. Job security is a thing of the past. The conventional measures of the welfare state do no longer work. Two kinds of response have emerged to this challenge: either more socialism or more capitalism.

Going on like in the past and more socialism would make things worse. The answer to the challenge is to abolish politics and the state. Selecting the legislators by sortition, the end of the state monopoly on money, and privatizing the system of justice and security, are the main steps to take. In as much as free capitalism would flourish, the costs of living fall, wage rates rise, incomes increase, and the burdens of taxation and bureaucracy fade away. The need to have a permanent job and a steady salary that is so urgent under the present system would vanish.

A libertarian revolution and an anarcho-capitalist order has become possible because the new technologies, with the Internet at its center, undermine the ability of the 'old regime' to maintain its hold over public opinion. Mind control by the modern state confronts the obstacle that the cost to engineer the public opinion outruns its effectiveness. New alternative sources of knowledge compete with the informational privilege of the government. The voice of the government has become one among many.

The necessity of an anarcho-capitalist order is not only a question of the material well-being. If we continue with the present system of governance, the state will grow bigger and bigger and become more totalitarian. In the hands of such a regime, the new technologies turn into deadly weapons against individual freedom.

In order to preserve and expand prosperity and liberty, establishing a libertarian system of governance has become a question of human survival.

The State and Its Minions

The State is generally considered as a necessity. Even many of those who believe that the State is an evil, regard it is a necessary evil. The State is indispensable, they say, only anarchist would dispute this fact.

Economic theory holds that the State is the provider of public and social goods. The public believes that the State is that organization by which we protect ourselves from ourselves. By subsidizing the supply of certain goods such as education and healthcare the State helps us to consume more of these benefits than we would do individually and with some harmful goods (the 'bads'), the State protects us against the damage that we would inflict upon ourselves if there were easy access to these products. There is a broad consensus that the State is necessary to provide things such as the roads, schools, hospitals, and care for our domestic and external security. Yet to be governed means more than just obtaining the supply of the so-called 'public goods', as Pierre-Joseph Proudhon indicts:

> *"To be GOVERNED is to be watched, inspected, spied upon, directed, law-driven, numbered, regulated, enrolled, indoctrinated, preached at, controlled, checked, estimated, valued, censured, commanded, by creatures who have neither the right nor the wisdom nor the virtue to do so. To be GOVERNED is to be at every operation, at every transaction noted, registered, counted, taxed, stamped, measured, numbered, assessed, licensed, authorized, admonished, prevented, forbidden, reformed, corrected, punished. It is, under pretext of public utility, and in the name of the general interest, to be place under contribution, drilled, fleeced, exploited, monopolized, extorted from, squeezed, hoaxed, robbed; then, at the slightest resistance, the first word of complaint, to be repressed, fined, vilified, harassed, hunted down, abused, clubbed, disarmed, bound, choked, imprisoned, judged, condemned, shot, deported, sacrificed, sold, betrayed; and to crown all, mocked, ridiculed, derided, outraged, dishonored. That is government; that is its justice; that is its morality."*
>
> (Pierre-Joseph Proudhon: *Idée Générale de la Révolution au XIXe Siècle* (1851)- General Idea of the Revolution in the Nineteenth Century.

More than 150 years late, things have not changed much. In a democracy, the State has not diminished its role but has grown into horrific dimensions as Hans-Hermann Hoppe describes in his "A Short History Of Man":

> *"Every detail of private life, property, trade, and contract is regulated...In the name of social, public, or national security, democratic caretakers "protect" us from global warming and cooling, the extinction of animals and plants and the*

depletion of natural resources, from husbands and wives, parents and employers, poverty, disease, disaster, ignorance, prejudice, racism, sexism, homophobia and countless other public "enemies" and "dangers. Yet the only task government was ever supposed to assume—of protecting our life and property—it does not perform. To the contrary, the higher the state expenditures on social, public, and national security have risen, the more private property rights have been eroded, the more property has been expropriated, confiscated, destroyed, and depreciated, and the more have people been deprived of the very foundation of all protection: of personal independence, economic strength, and private wealth. The more paper laws have been produced, the more legal uncertainty and moral hazard has been created, and lawlessness has displaced law and order. And while we have become ever more dependent, helpless, impoverished, threatened and insecure, the ruling elite of politicians and plutocrats has become increasingly richer, more corrupt, dangerously armed, and arrogant."

In a democracy, 'we' now are the State ourselves. The State is no longer separated from society, from the family, and from the local community but is in us, the people. "We are the State", the mob exclaims, fired up by the encouragements of the State's own band of cheerleaders. In a democracy, the State is not only necessary, it is we, our own identity.

A deeper analysis, however, reveals, that most of these popular claims are false. The State is not sacred. The State as the people is a fiction.

Along with Franz Oppenheimer in "The State" (1908), Murray Rothbard in his "The Anatomy of the State" (originally published in "Egalitarianism as a Revolt Against Nature and Other Essays" 1974) have thoroughly exploded the common justifications of the State.

As Rothbard points out in his essay, the identification of the people with the State leads to serious errors. Taking the State for the people provides the bases to claim that if "the government has incurred a huge public debt which must be paid by taxing one group for the benefit of another, this reality of burden is obscured by saying 'we owe it to ourselves', if the government conscripts a man, or throws him into jail for dissident opinion, he is 'doing it to himself', and, therefore, nothing untoward has occurred."

Also, in a democracy, the State is not 'we', the government is not 'us'. In a democracy, the "government does not in any accurate sense 'represent' the people".

What then, is the State, asks, Rothbard, if the State is not a family or an organ of which we are all part, and his answer is that "the State is that organization in the society which attempts to maintain a monopoly of the use of force and violence in a given territorial area; in particular, it is the only organization in a society that obtains its revenue not by voluntary contribution or payment of services and by the peaceful and voluntary sale of these goods and services to others, the State obtains its revenue by the use of compulsion, that is, by the use and the threat of the jailhouse and the bayonet."

In the footsteps of Joseph Schumpeter (*Capitalism, Socialism, and Democracy*, 1942), Rothbard extends the definition of the State by Max Weber as the "human community that (successfully) claims the monopoly of the legitimate use of physical force within a given territory" (in "*Politik als Beruf*" 1918) by the aspect that the Sate lives on a revenue which is produced in the private sphere for private purposes and must be taken away by political force.

Man is born into this world naked and helpless and of total dependence on care. It takes years for a human being to develop reasoning and to acquire the skills for production. Social association is a necessity in the early life and a requirement when grown up because the social cooperation within the network of the division of labor enhances the individual productivity. The exchange of goods is natural to man. When people exchange goods, they exchange property. Therefore, property rights and the free market exchange form a vital part of human nature.

As Franz Oppenheimer elaborates in '*Der Staat*' (1908), there are only two means of wealth accumulation: either through the economic mean or by political means. The political means are in the hands of the State. The State is the instrument to plunder the wealth of the private sector. The political instrument to acquire wealth is opposed to the economic way. While the economic method is natural and beneficial to all, the political way is unnatural and detrimental to the general prosperity. By means of the State, a few live at the cost of all. The basis of the political means is not a voluntary exchange but coercion. Not by a social contract comes the State into existence but with conquest and submission.

The State begins with conquest and has gone through a series of stages till our present days. As Oppenheimer recounts human history, the conquering tribe submits the conquered tribe in order to plunder. Yet instead of complete exploitation and elimination, the conquerors opt for a peaceful arrangement with the conquered. The conquerors unite with the conquered under the umbrella of a common State as a nation.

From the stateless society of the huntsmen and gatherers and the nomads and warriors, the State comes into existence with conquest and annihilation. Over time, the conquerors learn to exploit the conquered and use slavery and other forms of bondage instead of annihilation. Instead of getting the honey like a bear, the State acts like a beekeeper. From there emerges the territorial union of conquerors and conquered when the ruling class acts mainly as judicial supervisors and arbitrators for the conquered does finally merge with the people as a nation State. This stage prepares the path for the stateless society of the future, Oppenheimer predicts.

Historical Development Stages of the State
(based on The State by Franz Oppenheimer)

PREHISTORIC STATELESS SOCIETY	
STATELESS SOCIETY I	Huntsmen and gatherers
STATELESS SOCIETY II	Herdsmen and Vikings
STATELESS SOCIETY III	Nomads and warriors
STATE	
STAGE I	Conquest and annihilation of the conquered
STAGE II	Conquest and submission of the conquered
STAGE III	Capitalization and tribute extraction
STAGE IV	Territorial union
STAGE V	Rule by arbitration and courts
STAGE VI	Nation building
POST-HISTORIC STATELESS SOCIETY	
SELF-GOVERNING SOCIETY	Private law society
FREEMEN'S CITIZENSHIP	Demise of the state
ANARCHO-CAPITALISM	Voluntary exchange society

Economic development brings with it that the political means must recede against the economical means. Oppenheimer recognizes that in the political history of humankind there has been a steady ascent of the economic method at the cost of the political scheme. Writing at the beginning of the 20the century, Oppenheimer predicts that the thousands of years of State rule are coming to an end: "The 'state' of the future will be a 'society' guided by self-government", he declares.

So why is the State as an oppressive institution still here with us?

Why do we still have a State, asks Murray Rothbard, when the coercive and exploitive political means run against natural law? The political way is not productive but parasitic, "instead of adding to production, it subtracts from it". Parasitism is the nature of the State, also in its 'democratic' form. The State sucks wealth from the productive sector, it diminished the incentives to produce. The State makes us poor.

In the extension of the definitional approaches by Max Weber, Joseph Schumpeter, and Franz Oppenheimer, Murray Rothbard defines the State as "the systematization of the predatory process over a given territory". While private crime is sporadic and individual parasitism is ephemeral, and can be rejected by the victims, the State "provides a legal, orderly, systematic channel for the predation of private property; it renders certain, secure, and relatively 'peaceful' the lifeline of the parasitic caste in society".

As production comes before consumption, the provision of goods must precede their predation. The State cannot come into existence before the economy. Without the existence of an economy, there can be no 'social contract'. Without a productive basis, the social contract is a myth.

The State still exists. It has at its side the state apparatus and its officialdom. These, however, would not be enough if they were not expanded through State propaganda. Force is the *modus operandi* of the State but ideology provides the State's coherence. Even more so than in earlier times, governments need the consent of the ruled. As the welfare state approaches its economic limit, it becomes more difficult, to use the redistribution as the political means to gain mass loyalty. The group of people that receives net benefits from the State must be a minority. In order to gain the support of the majority, people must be persuaded by an ideology that government is necessary and inevitable, that it is benevolent and beneficial to all. In his "*Anatomy of the State*", Murray Rothbard identifies the modern intellectuals as the carriers of this task. The intellectuals as the opinion-makers serve as ideological bodyguards of the modern State.

The State and the intellectuals need one another. The State intellectuals are the priestly class of our days. The free market does not sustain many intellectuals. In order to gain a livelihood, they need the funding of the State. A historical alliance exists between the State and its intellectuals. Along with the officialdom, the intellectuals are the other leg how the State maintains its existence as a machinery of exploitation. Along with these allies, the modern secular State has also secured 'science' as its affiliate. While the priesthood decorated the State as holy, science deifies the State as the ultimate ratio. The bodyguards of the modern State are the host of experts that find ample employment in ministries, agencies, commissions, the universities, and at the plethora of national and international institutions.

Rothbard (1974) reveals that the "increasing use of scientific jargon has permitted the State's intellectuals to weave obscurantist apologia for State rule that would have only met with derision by the populace of a simpler age." These experts teach that the robbery by the State helps its victims, that the economy needs politics for its stabilization, and that employment and economic progress is the achievement of government. Under the mantle of science, the State has expanded like never before. It is now 'science' that serves as the apparatus of propaganda to promote the agenda for the expansion of the modern State. Exploitation has become so subtle that hardly anyone notices it anymore

The State protects itself and promotes its power by fear. If one foreign enemy is defeated, the next one is already chosen. Domestic enemies abound not only in a regime like Stalin's Soviet Union but also in the modern 'democracy'. The modern State itself is clad in the cloth of nationhood. The nation now serves as the source of passion, blind obedience, and the rationale of exclusion and condemnation of those individuals who will not succumb. The democratic State needs the nation because it is supposed to represent not the absolute king but the absolutism of the people.

As Hans-Hermann Hoppe (_A Short History of Men_, 2015) points out: "Under democracy the distinction between the rulers and ruled becomes blurred. The illusion even arises that the distinction no longer exists". Democracy transforms the limited wars of the past into the modern total wars where the enemy must be debased and dehumanized in favor of the glory of one's own nation.

The competition of political parties over votes is fundamentally different from competition in a market economy. In a market competition, producer compete as to the sale of their products against payment. In a democracy, politicians compete over votes in an exchange of favors. The apparent benefits that voters expect to receive consist of advantages as the result of coercive redistribution.

Driven by party politics, the democratic State moves inexorably towards its own demise. State bankruptcy looms across the globe. The social-democratic era is over. The capacity of the State to bribe is coming to an end. What to do after the collapse of the modern democratic State? The answer is anarcho-capitalism and the rule of a "_Private Law Society_" (Hoppe). In order to accomplish this change, the pre-condition is the separation between the intellectuals and the State in the same way as the separation of the Church and the State had brought down the old State. It is up to the academics to withdraw their endorsement of the State. The intellectuals have nothing to lose but their chains. The 'march through the institutions' is over. For those who study now, the road to ascendency through State service is closed.

Voluntary Servitude

In his essay on the politics of obedience (*Discours de la Servitude Volontaire*), Etienne La Boétie (1530-1563) asks the central question of political rule: How come that a people, as the majority, lets itself be ruled by a small group, the minority, and sometimes, in the case of an autocrat, falls into the hands of a single person? How is it possible that people permit that to a small group of men tortures, exploits and abuses the majority? Is it not strange, wonders La Boétie, that this dictatorial ruler, as a human, is often physically weak, clownish, feminine, cowardly and of a feeble mind?

Would it not rather be natural that one would obey one's parents as a child but after one has grown-up and gained reason, one would want to be nobody's servant and not the slave of someone else? La Boétie's answer to these questions is that the cause of human servitude cannot be only coercion. No tyrant has so many eyes that he could monitor a whole nation or have so many hands that he could hit the people with so many blows. The answer is obedience. Not coercion explains tyranny but 'voluntary servitude'.

Tyranny can come through elections, by force, or by inheritance. Although the methods differ about how the rulers come into power, the method of dominance is the same. All types of rules, including tyranny, are based on voluntary submission of the people. How did this bondage come about?

One reason is, La Boétie explains, that at some point in history human beings lost their freedom either by external conquest or internal corruption. Thereafter followed one generation after the other that no longer knew about freedom and what it means. Submission had become a habit. Men fell into servitude and became complacent in their condition of captivity. Human nature fell victim to the circumstances, to custom, to upbringing. Systematic state propaganda completed this process of subjection. Over time, the traces of the knowledge of freedom get lost and what has been left is only the experience of servitude as the natural way of human existence.

The second reason for servitude is resignation and diversion. Although servitude makes people uneasy, it also makes people calm in their resignation when other concerns than freedom occupies their mind. The rulers know that and provide the diversions of bread and circus, of gluttony and playfulness. The exhilaration that comes with the diversions that the mass culture delivers extinguishes defiance and the emotional exhaustion keeps the people still in their political resignation.

The third cause of submission is the tyrant's use of religion. People like to believe in miracles and the rulers search the décor that comes with ceremonies that celebrate divinity and holiness. The rulers create a web of taboos and sanctuaries. In tandem with the church service, there is the State service. This way, disobedience of the State becomes a sin, rebellion becomes an act of blasphemy, and tyrannicide becomes deicide.

As the fourth reason of voluntary servitude counts the role of a special class of persons who stand between the ruler and the people. These are the public employees, the state-financed intellectuals, and the rich who profit from the State. These people accept the bribe of the tyrant because they do not know better or because they esteem the benefits that they receive higher than their freedom and righteousness.

In a monarchy, as it was the case at the time when La Boétie lived, the courtiers and the nobility represented this group of the privileged. In the eyes of La Boétie, these persons are deplorable. These are people who have been abandoned by God and humanity, who humiliate themselves before the king and do not oppose the debasing treatment that they receive from their master. While the rest of the population obeys because it must do what told, those who form part of the entourage of the king or of the tyrant "have to think what the king wants them to think". These flatterers must anticipate the wishes of the autocrat and must please him. For them, to obey is not enough, they must adulate the tyrant. "Serving him destroys them, yet they are expected to share his joy, to abandon their tastes for his, to change their nature and constitution". The common people owe only a part of their existence to the tyrant, the sycophants all that they are and what they have.

Tyranny makes everybody suffer, including the tyrant himself. The autocrat can neither give nor receive love. He must not maintain friendship. He is surrounded by cruelty, dishonesty, and injustice.

What to do against this tragedy? How can mankind overcome submission? How can we get out of this scam and leave behind this calamity where everybody must suffer, including the tyrant himself? Let's forget the scholarly, convoluted answers, says La Boétie. The answer is plain. What needs to be done to avoid and to get rid of tyranny is the will and the desire of the individuals to remain free and to get free.

The gift of freedom is humankind's natural possession. It does not require justification or elaboration. All it takes is to reclaim one's freedom. Liberty is not a right but a choice. If it were a right, it could be taken away the same way that it was given. Yet freedom is not a right but a part of human nature. It belongs naturally to the human being. In his youthful optimism, Etienne exclaims: "Be determined to no longer be servants and you will be free." No other feat is required than just stop supporting the tyranny. Remove your support, and the colossus loses its stand and will tumble.

The pursuit of anarchy must not come by fire and rage. The tyrant needs not to be toppled from his throne by another man who becomes the new oppressor after his victory against the old. Throughout history, the consequence of the violent assault against tyranny has been that the leaders of the insurrection emptied the throne only to occupy it themselves. Conspiracies to do away with tyrants, tend to backfire and make matters worse. Insurgence is not the path to freedom.

It is not necessary to confront the tyrant. What needs to be done is removing the foundation of tyranny. Tyranny does not rest on force but on submission. To get rid of tyranny, people must stop their voluntary servitude. It is not the tyrant who puts himself into his position and stays in it but the people who submit to him. It is the people who feed the monster. People must stop to offer sacrifices, devotion, and idolatry, and the tyrant will fall on his own.

In order to end the tyranny of the State, people must stop accepting servitude. They need not take anything away from the tyrant, what they must do is stop yielding. To get out of tyranny, human beings do not need to change the essence of their nature. All one must do is to shed off what hinders individual advancement. When the tyrant does no longer receive obedience and people do no longer obey his orders, the ruler stands naked, without any power and is disarmed of the instruments of his dominance.

Without the support of the people, the tyrant is nothing. He shares the fate of a root that is left without water and nourishment: it turns into a dry, dead piece of wood: "Resolve to serve no more, and you are at once freed. I do not ask that you place your hands upon the tyrant to topple him over, but simply that you support him no longer, then you will behold him, like a great Colossus whose pedestal has been pulled away, fall of his own weight and break to pieces," says La Boétie. Learn anarchy, one may add.

Two centuries after La Boétie, in 1841, David Hume ("Of the First Principles of Government") put forth the same principle of servitude by consent with clarity and distinction:

> *"Nothing appears more surprising to those who consider human affairs with a philosophical eye, than the easiness with which the many are governed by the few; and the implicit submission, with which men resign their own sentiments and passions to those of their rulers. When we enquire by what means this wonder is effected, we shall find, that, as Force is always on the side of the governed, the governors have nothing to support them but opinion. It is therefore, on opinion only that government is founded, and this maxim extends to the most despotic and military governments, as well as to the most free and most popular."*

The story does not end here. While submission and voluntary servitude has been the rule, there will always be a few who feel the yoke of bondage and who will try to shake it off. Such people never will disappear completely from this earth, La Boétie claims: "Even if liberty had entirely perished from the earth, such men would invent it." The desire for freedom cannot be extinguished. Some extraordinary will always rekindle the light of freedom. Although they do not know freedom as a reality, they can imagine it and feel the spirit of liberty. These men, although robbed of their freedom, know that it does exist. Isolated from each other, each of them is lost in his own spiritual world, yet when they get the means to communicate with one another, the end of tyranny has come.

The Age of the Individual

The foremost exponent of the philosophy of anarcho-individualism is Max Stirner (1806-1856). In his "Der Einzige und sein Eigenthum" (Leipzig 1844/45) – "The unique one and his property", he claims that to come to oneself, one must get rid of the host of detrimental external influences that subdue and dissolve the essence of being one as oneself.

It is an obvious lie that man is born free. From birth to death, man forms part not only of society but of a specific society in time and space. For the anarcho-individualist, the human task is not to change society and exchange one power regime for the other. What matters is to liberate oneself from the society, to become oneself as much as one can. Egoism is not anti-social. By pursuing the path of egoism, one contributes - without intent - to a better society. Acting as a rational egoist promotes a better society. The best society is a stateless society composed of rational egoists.

Max Stirner diagnoses that the turn from the 18th to the 19th century marks the beginning of the "political epoch". The rupture came with the French Revolution. The State became the new God. People turned insane in their desires to serve this earthly God; the State cult became the new religion. Serving the State became the highest ideal of all and serving the State the highest honor of all.

Yet the State does not care about the individual, about what is me and what is mine. The State only cares about itself. The individual is nothing to the State; he is random to the State. For the State, the individual is nothing but a contingency. The point is that the State cannot understand the individual because the individual transcends the comprehension of the State. The concepts of the State, the understanding of the State, is too limited to comprehend an individual. Because the State cannot comprehend the individual, the State can do nothing for a man's individuality. The right attitude of the individual to the world is that he will do nothing because of God or because of humanity, but only because of himself.

The death of the old State and the abolition and containment of the monarchy did not liberate the individual. The democratic revolutions provoked the birth of politics and the worship of the State. The idea of the State entered the hearts of the people and aroused a new kind of enthusiasm: the national delirium. Serving the State as the new worldly God became a worship and the new cult. With the victory of classical liberalism, the epoch of the political began. To serve the State and its mystification as the nation became the supreme ideal, the interest of the State became the greatest interest and the civil service (even without being a civil servant) became the highest honor.

This historic fall marks the origin of the horrors of the modern world.

The protagonist of this new world is the politician and the political parties. A politician is a person whose aim is to change the people and the world by means of the State. Domination is the aim of the politician and the State apparatus is the instrument. The bigger and more effective the State, the better the State serves as a tool of suppression and control. The force of the State is universal to the politician – only comparable to God's power. The desire of the politician is the omnipotent State no less than the almightiness of the holy Lord.

Yet in doing so and take the State as his tool, the politician suffers from a great illusion. The State is neither the most comprehensive nor the most effective instrument of control of the individual although the government apparatus is the most visible machine of dominance. Furthermore, in as much as the politician wants to dominate and rule, he himself is under the authority of his own political party. Therefore, being a politician means being unfree. As a member of a political party, the politician must adopt the credo of the party, he must follow the rules of the party and he has to adhere to the party's principles. The truth is that the political party owns the politician. The people know that the politician is a fake because while he pretends to set the rules and to be the master, he himself is the system's deplorable victim.

Politicians do and cannot represent the individual. They have the State in their heads and in their hearts. Politicians do not believe in the individual, they believe in the State. Politicians are possessed by the State, they are "State-believers" and therefore politicians are the enemies of the individual. The politicians evoke the "common good" as their goal. Yet the idea of a "common good" is an illusion. "The common good is not my good", writes Stirner, "The common good cheers, while I suffer– the State shines, while I languish."

Liberalism did not unfetter the individual. "Liberalism" is the application of rational insight to our issues, and thus the aim of liberalism is a "rational order", a "moral conduct", and a "limited liberty". Liberalism opposes anarchy, lawlessness, proper individuality, and in as much as rationality rules, the individual person becomes a subject. Under liberalism, the individual is not his own master. Reason should prevail, says liberalism, also at the cost of the individual and to the detriment of the peculiarities of a person's personality. Instead of an era of freedom, the victory of classical liberalism marks the beginning of the 'epoch of the political'.

Individualist anarchism is the way to overcome the horrors of the modern State. Anarcho-individualism comes into existence as the association of rational egoists. Egoism is different from egotism or brutish selfishness. Rational egoism is not hedonism. The rational egoist is prudent, his mind is balanced. He abhors the immediate gratification that comes with passion and pleasure. The rational egoist is not egotistical and not anti-social. Society as an association of rational egoists requires no ruler. The commercial society exists as voluntary exchange relations. The rational egoist does neither need nor want a ruler. In the same way, as he rejects government, the rational egoist rejects the other rulers that may dominate him such as the greed for money, power, and fame.

Not the individual egoist is egotistical, but the truly egotistical entities are the collectives, such as the nation, the family, the church, and the State. While the egoism of the individual is natural, the egotism of these collectives is artificial. While the egoism of the individual is restrained, the egotism of the collectives is limitless. Collectives may claim altruism, yet their genuine identity is the application of moral terrorism as the way to maintain themselves. While a rational egoist may voluntarily act altruistically under specific circumstances as it serves his wants, a collective, in contrast, will apply moral pressures to force its members to give up their own interests in favor the so-called common good of the collective. Collectives are brutal egotistical entities, and the coldest, harshest, most brutal of all collectives is the State. The State is that peculiar institution, which systematically combines moral terror with physical force.

There is a permanent conflict between the individual and the collective. The individual and the collective are natural enemies. The individual is a coincidence of the collective. The collective looks only after itself while the individual must take care of his own. The individual's interest is in himself, yet the collective wants all for itself and nothing for the individual. The collective demands self-denial and wants to keep the individual as its subject. Yet the individual wants himself and nothing else than himself.

The power of the collective is the powerlessness of the individual. The humility of the individual is the sovereignty of the collective. The collective rules through the resignation of the individuals. The despondency of the individual provides the courage of the collective to demand the submissiveness of the individual under the authority of the collective. Everything that one, as an individual, can be, one does become not through the collective but against the collective.

Collectives exert moral oppression. Their tools are the false gods of duty, pride, and sacrifice. Yet different from the association of rational egoists, the collective does not give compensation. The pattern of exchange in the collective is not reciprocity but extraction. Of all collectivist entities, the most horrific is the State. The State is the most suppressive and the most dangerous collective and therefore the greatest enemy of the individual because the State is the collective with the most comprehensive access to the application of violence. The modern State is the greatest propagator of modern wretchedness. The modern alienation is not the result of the division of labor but results from the individual's submission under the all-encompassing power of the State.

The State is the great trickster of the modern era. The politicians promise justice, freedom, and equality and in return demand all the power for themselves in the form of getting hold of the State power. By promising all, the State then takes all and makes the individual powerless. For the State, the claim to legality is the claim to violence. Law is created by State power yet a right that is bestowed is not a right and a type of freedom that is not achieved by oneself is not freedom. Justice is an instrument of tyranny and social justice is the tool of absolute tyranny. Equality is the biggest of all State lies. The desire for equality is already fraudulent, claims Max Stirner.

The way out of the captivity under the modern State is the free association of egoists beyond the State. However, under the present system of a comprehensive State, one cannot expect that many people will find their way to themselves. Most people will only become aware of their individuality when the collectivist bondage has ended and when the State is gone.

There will be not freedom as long as there exist a State. Doing away with the State is the great challenge of our time. In a dialectical turn of Hegelian dimension, the abolishment of the State is a political act. Ending the State may be the last and the greatest collective feat, the last and the greatest achievement of politics and it may be the true historical mission of political parties.

Rational egoism as it is promoted by Max Stirner must need be confounded with psychological and ethical egoism. Rational egoism is thoughtful self-interest, while psychological egoism is pathological. Ethical egoism is also off the screen of Stirner's concept of egoism because it would imply a moral obligation, which goes completely against the thrust of the philosophy of Max Stirner.

Types of egoism

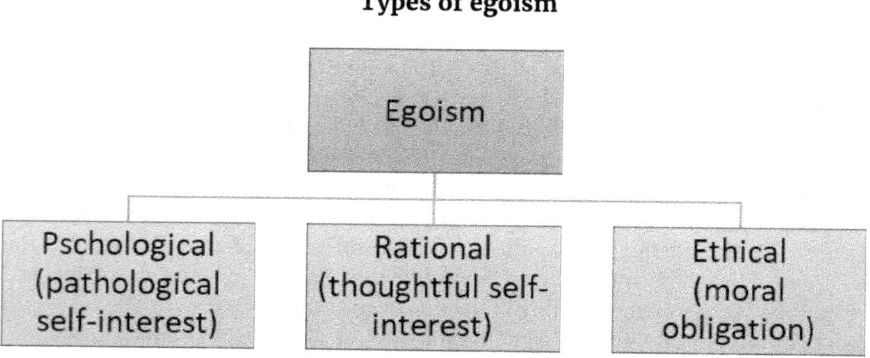

What Is Anarchism?

When we go beyond the mere explication of the concept 'anarchism' as one of Greek origin composed of '*an*' (against) and '*arkhos*' (leader), things get somewhat confused because 'anarchism' is also a political term, and as all political terms it is a polemical concept. In the sense of 'absence of government', the term emerged in France in the 1530s as '*anarchie*' and from the 1660s onwards, it was used as a general expression for the absence of authority and of a state of confusion. With the emergence of philosophers who called themselves explicitly 'anarchist', the term gained its modern meaning in the first half of the 19th century as 'order without power', 'stateless society', and 'direct government'.

Some historians of anarchism will trace back the roots of anarchism to Laozi, the ancient Greeks and the Stoics, while others will locate the origin of anarchism in the decades following the French Revolution. As a concept, too, 'anarchism' is many-layered. Much more than a specific term, anarchism is a generic concept which encompasses a wide range of meanings and many contradictions.

Whatever is the purpose of a classification, a necessary distinction must be made between 'political' and 'philosophical' anarchism. There is little that these two have in common and it may even appear doubtful whether the 'political anarchists' may have a legitimate claim on the title of 'anarchist'. After all, 'political anarchism' means being involved in political action ranging from public agitation to participate in wars (as it happened in the Spanish civil war with the syndicalist anarchists). The representatives of political anarchism such as Pierre-Joseph Proudhon (1809-1865), Mikhail Bakunin (1814-1876), and Peter Kropotkin (1842-1921) took an active part in the political fights of their days and were not less belligerent than their Communist soulmates.

Something else puts the political anarchist also close to their Communist brethren: their demand for economic equality. In this respect, the 'political anarchists' commit the same error as the Communists because they ignore that inequality lies in the nature of man and efforts of making something equal which is naturally unequal requires force and therefore is profoundly anti-anarchistic. More so, by participating in the political battles, the political anarchists betray the anarchist principle of opposing politics. What else is politics than the fight about gaining control of the State apparatus?

Sadly enough, the most widely distributed books about anarchism, such as, for example, Colin Ward's "Anarchism", which appeared in the Oxford series of "very short introductions" (Colin Ward: *Anarchism. A Very Short Introduction*. Oxford University Press 2004), largely ignore the difference between political and philosophical anarchism and dedicate almost all of their considerations to political anarchism. Ward stands in the tradition of other writers about anarchism such as George Woodcock's 470-page book, *Anarchism* of 1962, which has enjoyed many reprints as a Penguin paperback and was translated into many languages. Likewise, Peter Marshall's treatise of more than 700 pages called _Demanding the Impossible: A History of Anarchism_ (HarperCollins) of 1992 which enjoys a large readership, does not provide a deep analysis of the philosophical branch of anarchism.

Philosophical anarchism is different from the political anarchism not because it is passive but because it does not choose the political way of bringing about an anarchist order. The philosophical anarchists know that throughout history the forceful replacement of one ruler has only emptied the chair for the next to take the seat of power. The philosophical anarchists also know that dominance does not come from force but by the consent of the dominated. The right way to proceed, therefore, is not confrontation with the State power but removing one's support from the State. The philosophical anarchists follow the insight that it is public opinion that produces voluntary servitude and that submission makes tyranny possible. The task of the philosophical anarchist is enlightenment, not rebellion. The political anarchist's way is more like a mutiny than an uprising.

The path to a free society comes through the change of public opinion. While this way seems long, shortcuts are not an alternative because they lead nowhere and most of the time only bring setbacks in the battle for liberty. Changes of opinion happen in an exponential form. For a long time, it may seem as if there hardly is any progress. Yet as time goes by, the curve gets steeper and finally things change overnight. Philosophical anarchists face only themselves as their foe when they desist and resign.

Different from the political anarchism which emerged in the decades after the French Revolution, philosophical anarchism can be traced back to the pre-Christian era. The time-line of thinkers in this tradition is impressive. Philosophical anarchism can claim the Chinese Laozi (who died in 533 BC) as one of their earliest known representatives of an anti-authoritarian political philosophy ('In governing, don't try to control'), the Greek school of the cynics and the stoics as well as the many elements of anarchistic thinking in Buddhism and Hinduism.

Zeno of Citium, in the footsteps of Diogenes of Sinope, advocated anarchistic forms of society around 300 BC. Zeno's model of a Republic needs no State structures. In opposition to Plato (ca. 425 BC to 348/347 BC), Zeno opposed the omnipotence of the State, contra its intervention and its regimentation. He argued that man's natural sociability keeps his egoism in check.

Better known than Zeno and Diogenes are the writings of Epicurus (341 BC to 270 BC). Following the atomic materialism of Democritus, the philosophy of Epicurus opposes superstition and divine intervention. As the original thinker of what nowadays is called "epicureanism", he promoted hedonism and for that opposed participation in politics because of its connection to the lust for power and to the desire for fame.

Ancient Rome was the very anti-thesis to anarchism. The stoics Epictetus (50 to 135) and Marcus Aurelius (121-180) are the few thinkers in ancient Rome with some connection to anarchism.

We do not know which philosopher had lived in the commercial realm of Carthage and contributed to anarchist thought. In the three Punic Wars (264 BC to 146 BC), the Roman militarism wiped out Carthage with only a heap of stones left. The Carthaginian commercial empire was one of the economically highest developed communities, a fully commercial commonwealth with strong anarcho-capitalist characteristics. Maybe the Carthaginians had no libertarian or anarchist philosopher because they did not need them as they were already the practitioners of a stateless society.

In the Middle Ages, Meister Eckhart (ca. 1260 – ca. 1328) rose to prominence as a theologian and mystic. His writings had a great influence on the thinking of the communitarian anarchist Gustav Landauer (1870-1919), who in turn inspired the early Zionist kibbutz movement.

Concerning the philosophy of late Middle Ages, one must pay tribute to the great contributions of the Portuguese and Spanish scholastics, particularly the works of Francisco Suárez (1548-1617), with the promotion of concepts such as subjective utility, personal sovereignty, and the justification of tyrannicide.

In the wake of the Reformation, several anarchist movements of Christian character appeared such as Hussites, Adamites and the early Anabaptists. Known as the "Münster Rebellion", the Anabaptists established a short-lived communal sectarian government in 1534 which was crashed down in 1535.

At the beginning of the modern age, the first great master pieces of anti-authoritarian thinking were "The Praise of Folly" (1511) by Erasmus of Rotterdam (1466-1536), followed by "Voluntary Servitude" (written around 1549, published in 1576) by Etienne La Boétie (1530-1563). Both are classics that have not lost any of their relevance.

A milestone in the development of libertarian thinking and anarcho-philosophy came with the publication of *"The Grumbling Hive, or Knaves Turn'd Honest"* in 1705, better known under its later title as *"Fable of the Bees. Private Vices, Publick Benefits"* by Bernard de Mandeville (1670-1733). Without this intellectual breakthrough, this profound transformation of moral values, neither the economic theories of Adam Smith nor the philosophical ideas of David Hume would have come forth, and all of these three have motivated Immanuel Kant (1724-1804) to write his promotion of the world peace of a community of free republics with his *"Toward an Eternal Peace"* (1795).

A proper anarchist literature emerges with William Godwin (1756-1836) who uses the term anarchism with adroit. His *"Enquiry Concerning Political Justice and its Influence on Morals and Happiness"* of 1793 is a classic of anarchist literature. In this work, Godwin denounces the State as the institution that instead of its claim of promoting human progress, restrains the advancement of mankind.

With a grain of salt, one may add to this chronology John Stuart Mill (1805-1873), particularly his *On Liberty* (1859). It is not completely false when some authors name Mill as the founder of what nowadays in American usage is called "liberalism" and elsewhere is known as "social democracy".

The first treatise on individualist anarchism was written by Max Stirner (1806-1856). His *"Der Einzige und sein Eigenthum"* (not quite correctly translated as '*The Ego and its Own*') was published in 1844 (predated to 1845). His philosophy is a radical denouncement of all collectives that terrorize the individual as spooks in the form of abstractions, such as God, the nation, or society.

Individualist anarchism flourished in the 19th century in the United States in the works of such well-known figures as Ralph Waldo Emerson (1803-1882), William Graham Sumner (1840-1910), Benjamin Tucker (1854-1939) and continued to prosper in the 20th century with authors such as Murray Rothbard (1926-1995), Robert Nozick (1938-2002) and many more.

The Austrian School of Economics stands in close connection with the anarchist tradition in the United States. Many libertarian scholars are also Austrian economists such as Murray Rothbard. Austrian economics has its roots in the scholarly contributions of Carl Menger (1840-1921), Eugen von Böhm-Bawerk (1851-1914), Ludwig von Mises (1881-1973), and Friedrich Hayek (1899-1992). This school, in turn, can trace its roots back to the school of Salamanca and the French economists such as Francois Quesnay (1694-1774), Anne Robert Jacques Turgot (1727-1781), Jean-Baptiste Say (1767-1832), and Frédéric Bastiat (1801-1850).

Timeline of modern anarchism

Type	Representative	Major work(s)	Quote
Liberal Anarchism	William Godwin (1756-1836)	*Enquiry concerning Political Justice, and its Influence on General Virtue and Happiness (1793)*	'Government was intended to suppress injustice, but its effect has been to embody and perpetuate it.'
Ego-Anarchism	Max Stirner (1806-1856)	*The Ego and Its Own (1844)*	*'What is freedom? To have the will to be responsible for one's self.'*
Mutualism	Pierre-Joseph Proudhon (1809-	*What is Property? (1840)*	'Property is theft' 'Property is

	1865)		freedom' 'Anarchy is order'
Socialist Anarchism	Mikhail Bakunin (1814-1876)	*God and the State (1882)*	'Freedom without socialism is privilege and injustice, but socialism without freedom is slavery and brutality.'
Anarcho-Syndicalism	Rudolf Rocker (1873-1958)	*Nationalism and Culture (1937)* *Anarcho-Syndicalism: Theory & Practice (1947)*	'it is the state which creates the nation, and not the nation the state.'
Communist Anarchism	Peter Kropotkin (1842–1921)	*Fields, Factories and Workshops (1899)*	'All things are for all' 'Don't compete!'
Communal Anarchism	Gustav Landauer (1870-1919)	*Revolution (1907)*	'nothing but the rebirth of all peoples out of the spirit of regional community can bring salvation'
Feminist Anarchism	Emma Goldman (1869-1940)	*Anarchism and Other Essays (1910)*	"I demand the independence of woman, her right to support herself; to live for herself; to love whomever she pleases, or as many as she pleases.'
Individualist	Benjamin Tucker	Individual	'Mind your own

Anarchism	(1854-1939)	Liberty, 1926	business' 'Aggression, invasion, government, are interconvertible'
Anarcho-liberalism (libertarianism)	Murray Rothbard (1826-1995)	*The Ethics of Liberty* (1982)	'Government is a band of thieves writ large'
Anarcho-capitalism	Hans-Hermann Hoppe (1849-)	*Democracy - the God that Failed*	'Democracy has nothing to do with freedom'

***

It does not matter whether one believes in God or in natural selection as long as one sticks to the principle that both, individuality and sociability, are inherent to human nature and therefore no external force is needed for the individual to live and prosper together with other individuals in a community. Anarchism is the freedom from external control beyond that which comes from oneself. Anarchism is anti-state and anti-government, but not anti-social. Because laws are only justified when they are in harmony with human nature, no State legislation is needed. The laws that are justified by nature need no codification and all other laws are illegitimate.

Anarchism is radical individualism. The theory of anarchism rejects the reality of collectives and adheres to a strict nominalism. Collectives such as the State or the Church are real only insofar as they form part of an individual's belief system.

The common body of anarchism is the pursuit of liberty not in the State and under the State or as the State, but against State and government. Anarchist reject the ancient Roman concept of *libertas* as a republican constitution of a popular government, the Lockean concept of liberty as individual liberty protected by the State or the concept of liberty as *volonté général* by Rousseau or liberty as embodied in the rationality of statehood as in Hegel's philosophy.

Types of Anarchism

The distinction between political and philosophical anarchism is important because it is only partially a separation between politics and theory as it is common also in other areas, such as in economics, for example. As to anarchism, the distinction refers also to the method of how to establish an anarchist society. The way for the political anarchists is political activism, the launch of political parties and the use of direct political exploits. Philosophical anarchists, in contrast, want to bring about the anarchist society through indirect means, through the change of public opinion and by incremental privatizations. The method of the political anarchist is political and confrontational; the method of the philosophical anarchists is persuasive and economic.

Anarcho-syndicalism seeks to establish an anarchist society through the mobilization of the working class. In this sense, this movement is an immediate rival of the Communists who claim to have the same 'revolutionary subject' as their vehicle. It comes as no surprise that the competition between these two groups has been fierce and combative. In the great political battles of the past century, the anarcho-syndicalists were frequently the enemy of both the Communists and the social democrats. In the trenches of the Spanish civil war, the factions of the political anarchism were as much fighting against each other as against the fascists as their common enemy.

Collectivist anarchism shares the Communist ideal of common property but is opposed to the rule of a party. The main representatives of the collectivist anarchism, such as Peter Kropotkin, were rancorous enemies of the Soviet regime as it was established under Vladimir Lenin in 1917. Collectivist anarchism made important contributions to the kibbutzim communities of the Zionist movement during the foundational period of Israel.

The main representatives of philosophical anarchism are individualist anarchism and anarcho-capitalism. The very designation as 'individualist' already prohibits for this line of thinking that one would form political parties or fight together in partisan groups. It would be wrong, however, to classify the individualist anarchist as solitary or anti-social. Not even the most radical of this line of thinking, Max Stirner, called to abandon community and social cooperation. His ideal was an 'association of egoists', where one egoism matches that of the others, and all members profit from social exchange and the division of labor.

Anarcho-capitalism is based on economics. The major difference to the other forms of anarchism is that anarcho-capitalist does promote neither common property nor equality of income and wealth. Anarcho-capitalism demands free markets as extensive and as intensive as possible based on the respect for private property. The theory of anarcho-capitalism holds that under the condition of free capitalism, differences in wealth and income will emerge only temporarily for specific producers and will be wiped-out sooner or later because of technical progress and free market entry. Furthermore, anarcho-capitalism postulates that under the conditions of free competition with low barriers to market entry and market exit, technological progress will happen more rapidly, more frequently, and rather continually so that the disruptive effect of change will be smaller than it is in a more slow-moving society where social and political interests have time to gain power positions and where habit makes people conformist.

For the anarcho-capitalist, freedom and prosperity have their anchor in private property. This way, Hans-Hermann Hoppe explains the Rothbardian ethics:

> *"Everyone is the proper owner of his own physical body as well as of all places and nature-given goods that he occupies and puts to use by means of his body, provided only that no one else has already occupied or used the same places and goods before him. This ownership of "originally appropriated" places and goods by a person implies his right to use and transform these places and goods in any way he sees fit, provided only that he does not change thereby uninvitedly the physical integrity of places and goods originally appropriated by another person. In particular, once a place or good has been first appropriated by, in John Locke's phrase, 'mixing one's labor' with it, ownership in such places and goods can be acquired only by means of a voluntary – contractual – transfer of its property title from a previous to a later owner."*

A problem shared by all variants of anarchism is the problem that freedom exists in a trilateral field of tension. A look at the dimensions of freedom makes it clear that full liberty is beyond human ability. There will never be complete 'freedom of' or 'freedom to'. The best one can hope to achieve is a high degree of 'freedom from', such as the freedom from tyranny and the freedom from misery.

Dimensions of Freedom

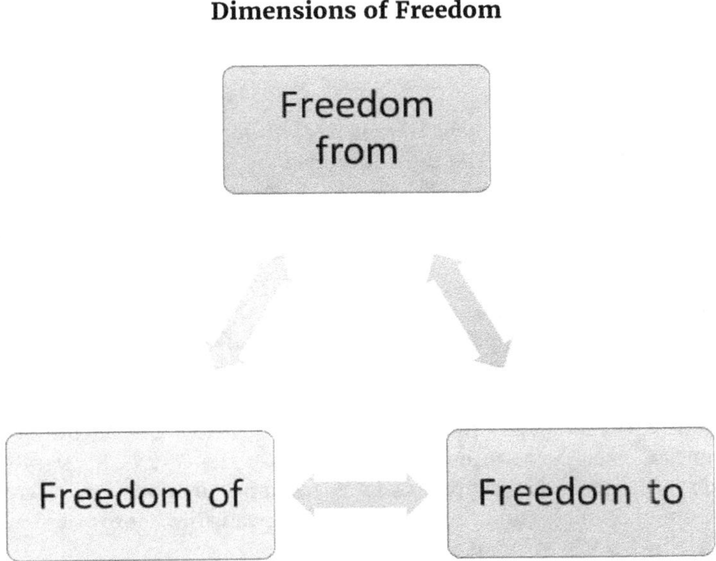

After the disaster of the Spanish Civil War for the political anarchist movement, political anarchism has lost much of its appeal. Even the kibbutzim movement has largely petered out. Fascism, Nazism, and Communism have gone, and with it political anarchism as their main counterpunch. What lives on and has gained more momentum since the beginning of the second half of the 20th century is philosophical anarchism, both as individualist anarchism and as anarcho-capitalism. There is no mutual exclusion between individualist anarchism and anarcho-capitalism. Each line of thinking stresses a somewhat different point. Individualist anarchism focuses primarily on the 'freedom to' - to be one's own personality as one wishes to develop. Both, anarcho-capitalism and individualist anarchism, demand the 'freedom of', such as the freedom of speech and both claim as much 'freedom from' as possible in the sense of freedom from tyranny and economic misery.

***

The books were on the shelf, the knowledge spread, yet the time had not yet come in the past centuries to realize the utopia of a free society. The political means was still too powerful compared to the economic means, as the famous distinction put forward by Franz Oppenheimer says.

In his book about voluntary servitude, Etienne La Boétie lamented that even under the worst suppression by tyranny, there will always be some eminent men who know about freedom, who feel the spirit of liberty but with censorship, difficulties of transport, and the means of communication under State control, these freedom-minded persons have a hard time communicating and remain solitary in their efforts.

In our times, these conditions have changed. The restraints on communication and transport have diminished. All it takes is to maintain and gain back the right of free speech. The right to bear guns as the armament of the people against tyranny is not sufficient without the freedom of speech. These two rights belong together, and it is not a coincidence that they stand side by side as the first and second amendment of the American Constitution.

Today, the main task of the philosophical anarchist is his engagement for free speech because it is the only way how a change of public opinion can come about. Different from the State intellectuals, the philosophical anarchists will not manipulate. Their use of the media is not to indoctrinate the people. It is the creed of the philosophical anarchists that liberty is not a chimera, that it is not something that comes from the outside to the hearts of the men but that it is within everybody, that it is not an attachment to human nature but at the core of his very existence. Free speech is the means to express oneself, to distinguish oneself, to speak about one's wishes and of one's conditions. Free speech means human expression. Without free speech, the essence of being a human gets lost.

The only way to extinguish the human strife for liberty is to suppress free speech. As long as the freedom of expression is with us, the freedom of man is safe. So long as we can speak up freely, the light of liberty will shine, and the message of freedom will spread.

Is Anarcho-Capitalism Possible?

Even if one agrees that anarcho-capitalism has become a necessity, the question arises whether such a governance is possible. After all, at first sight, insurmountable problems seem to prevent the flourishing of a stateless society. Libertarianism means a private law society. Private businesses in the marketplace provide the traditional functions of the state. An order of anarcho-capitalism substitutes the hierarchical coordination of activities of the state through horizontal cooperation based on voluntary exchange. Although a libertarian order amounts to a revolution as to its consequences, the path to its creation is non-revolutionary. The way to an anarcho-capitalist order is gradual as an on-going process of privatizations. Beginning with the sale of semi-public enterprises and public utilities, privatization will extend step by step to education and health and will also encompass security and the judicial system.

Frequent objections against anarcho-capitalism doubt the possibility to substitute state activity by the private sector. Questions arise such as: 'If there is no state, who would build the roads - who would care for the poor - who would provide for education, health services, security, and justice? If there is no state, who would pay the pensions?' - Such questions are not the result of analysis but of habit. If the supply of socks and underwear were in the hands of the state, people would ask the same questions concerning socks and underwear. If the state takes over an activity, it drives out private supply. This leads to the paradoxical result that government services seem indispensable the more activities the state has under its control.

Not too long ago, many of the activities, which now provides the state, were in private hands. The government did not take over these services because the private sector failed but because the party politicians, in their search for power and its extension, have encroached upon the private sector. Once when the interventionist spiral got started, there was no end: the more the state commands, the mightier politicians and state functionaries become. As the market economy recedes, the easier it gets for the party politicians to bring further activities under their authority.

When the state takes over an economic activity, scarcity does not diminish but grows. Therefore, all major activities of the state - be it education, healthcare or external and domestic security - appear always as being under-funded and in need of expansion. Because of the artificial scarcity, the electorate demands more of these services the more the state provides. No party politicians would dare to deny these wishes. Which political party representative would propose less spending for education, healthcare, and security? The voters do not realize that they are in a trap. They fail to see that beyond the lack of efficiency there is also an oversupply of governmental services.

The limit to an endless expansion of the state in terms of expenditures is the budget constraint. When the state has reached the financial limit, the control mania does not stop but goes on in other areas. When government spending hits its bound and financial restrictions curtail government expenditures, the state turns to the control of those activities that do not require spending money. Consequently, the fastest growing areas of state activities over the past decades have been behavioral sanctions - reaching from what one may eat and drink to what one may say and not say. First, governments regulate what you may take into your mouth, then the state controls what may come out of your mouth.

Under anarcho-capitalism, most of what the state supplies in services could fall to a fraction of the present volume. On a world-wide scale, military spending alone comprises around 1.7 trillion US-dollars annually. The so-called 'public services' would not only become better and cheaper, but it would also turn out that under a free market, the demand for education, healthcare, defense, and domestic security would be much different than it is now. Therefore, to privatize many of the activities, which now are under the authority of state would not only lead to a decrease of the costs per unit of the services but also reduce the volume of supply because a large part of the current supply of so-called 'public goods' is a useless waste. Losing none of the genuine benefits of education, healthcare, and defense, the budgets for these provisions could fall to a fraction of their present size.

If one includes the overblown judicial and public administration apparatus into the reduction of state activity, government spending, which nowadays is close to fifty percent of the gross domestic product in most industrialized countries, could come down to the single digits. Taxes and contributions could fall by ninety percent.

Different from what is presently the dominant belief, to privatize the police functions and the judiciary is not such a big problem. It would mean to extend what is already going on. In the United States of today, for example, private policing, such as by security guards, happens already at a grand scale and comprises more than one million persons. In some countries, including the United States, the number of private police and security already exceeds the number of official policemen. The private provision of judicial services is on the rise. Arbitration courts experience a strong and increasing demand including services for cross-border disputes. These trends will go on because private protection and arbitration is cheaper and better than the public provision. In Brazil, for example, which entertains one of the most expensive judicial systems of the world, currently about eighty million cases are pending without decision, and legal uncertainty has become monstrous.

The Struggle for Liberty

Some critics of libertarianism ask that if anarcho-capitalism were such a good order, why hasn't it been tried before. The answer to that contention is that there has not yet been a libertarian order because up to now it was impossible to have one. The cause for this is that throughout history, regimes established themselves by force and as soon as a specific person or group of persons had conquered power, they would try to monopolize information to their favor. Bereft of means of communication and under censorship, libertarianism was denied its voice in contrast to the avalanche of theories, opinions, and propaganda that justified and deified the state and government.

Throughout history, information was a monopoly. Most the people could not read or write. Books, pamphlets, and other reading material were beyond the reach of the common man. It was only in the 15th century when a significant change took place with the printing press based on moveable letters. This business innovation lowered the costs of publications. As reading material became accessible, learning to read and to write became a useful skill.

Inventing the modern printing press ended the era of a monopoly of information. Yet this technology was still too limited to bring a full inclusion. What came about was not universality of information but an informational oligopoly. Over the past centuries, a few institutions held the power in their hands. A small group of newspapers, publishing houses, universities and a few relevant TV stations, and film studios have controlled the media and guaranteed the role of a few powerful states and global institutions as the holders of power. This situation is about to change, and the conversion will be as dramatic as that which happened with the shift from the monopolistic age of information to an oligopolistic structure.

Before Johannes Gutenberg invented the printing press with mobile letters in the first half of the 15thcentury, information was a monopoly business. Access to information and its distribution confronted high barriers to entry. For those outside the dominant power structure, it was impossible to overcome these fences. Since technological thresholds restricted the access to and the use of information, it was easy for those in power to control the content and the access to information. Control over information means dominance over people. This constellation established a power system which excluded large parts of the population. When these informational barriers fell, the world began to change like never before.

The first manifestations of the new oligopolistic structure of information was the rise of religious groups outside Catholicism. It is no exaggeration to say that without the modern printing press, neither the Reformation nor the scientific revolution, nor the industrial revolution, could have happened. The modern 'knowledge economy' begins with the printing press because this instrument was essential for the dissemination of knowledge beyond small circles.

The modern age did not yet bring full liberty. The world as it emerged from the fifteenth century onward has remained a world of authoritarian power and control. While the old monopoly structure disappeared, not freedom, but an oligopoly emerged, which allowed censorship and exclusion although in a more limited way than had been the case in the age of the monopoly of information.

It was not only in the religious sphere that an oligopoly supplanted the monopoly, but also in the sphere of politics and science. In almost all its aspects, the modern world presents these oligopolistic structures. For example, there is not much more than about a handful of countries that represent the great powers, as it is institutionalized with the permanent members of the Security Council of the United Nations or the G7. Almost the same oligopolistic structure holds for scientific theories, with dominant ideologies or with the group of prestigious universities. Conflicts did not abate but rose because it had become more difficult to establish a monopoly of information. A fierce struggle among the oligopoly of states, parties, scientific theories, ideologies, and religions characterizes the modern age. Not an era of freedom and peace emerged but a period of atrocious struggles between the members of the various oligopolies with each one striving to become a monopolist.

Now, with the new information technologies, this strife of the members of the oligopoly of becoming the monopolist is falling apart because the new informational landscape has gained a polypolistic structure where not a few participants struggle but many suppliers compete with no one having a chance to dominate the market.

***

With the onset of the industrial revolution, the fight for lower taxes became the main content of the American and the French revolution with the consequent abolishment of the monarchy. Yet doing away with the monarchy did not mean doing away with the state. Libertarian philosophy experienced its first great flourishing at the time of the American Revolution. In continuation of the thoughts and theories of classical liberalism, American pamphleteers popularized liberty and of a state-free economy and prepared the path for the American independence.

Classical liberalism wanted to promote individual liberty and to minimize and to do away with the state as the enemy of individualism and liberty. The political program of the old liberalism called for the lowest level of taxes and wanted to eliminate economic regulations. The aim of liberalism was to set the individual free from the shackles and burdens of the traditional state and its absolutist and authoritarian encroachments. A break-up between the alliance of the throne with the merchants and the church was the intention of liberal movement. Separating these spheres meant to diminish the role of government and of the state-aligned church. Along with promoting peace, an essential part of the liberal project was to reduce the size and power of the state. The main weapon of the liberals in the battle against the state was the fight for lower taxes.

Yet the time was not yet ripe for the full establishment of an anarcho-capitalist order and of the reign of the 'obvious and simple system of natural liberty' as Adam Smith put it. Together with classical liberalism in England, American libertarianism came under the authority of the state as the promoter of what nowadays is called 'liberalism'. This modern liberal - or rather 'social-democratic'- political structure is far removed from the original ideas of classical liberalism and in some respects, it is the opposite. Instead of having less state, liberal democracy comes with more intervention; instead of more individual liberty, the current system has extended its control over the individual.

Even those countries that had gotten rid of the monarchy, suffered from the restoration of the state.

Murray Rothbard ("For a New Liberty. The Libertarian Manifesto p. 12) explains that in the 19th century "*statism and Big Government returned, but this time displaying a preindustrial and pro-general-welfare face. The Old Order returned, but this time the beneficiaries were shuffled a bit; they were not so much the nobility, the feudal landlords, the army, the bureaucracy, and privileged merchants as they were the army, the bureaucracy, the weakened feudal landlord, and especially the privileged manufacturer. Led by Bismarck in Prussia, the New Right fashioned a right-wing collectivism based on war, militarism, protectionism, and the compulsory cartelization of business and industry - a giant network of controls, regulations, subsidies, and privileges which forged a great partnership of Big Government with certain favored elements in big business and industry.*"

Compared to the monarchical rule, things got worse. The new 'democratic' states would not only more spend, tax, and regulate but also become more aggressive. The democratic revolutions gave birth to three poisonous monsters: nationalism, imperialism, and socialism.

In as much as the masses had to be convinced that this new interventionist nationalist state was better for the people than a minimal state and free markets, to manipulate public opinion would now play a central role. With the demise of the churchmen as the main molders of public creed came the rise of the modern intellectual: "*the new breed of professors, Ph.D's, historians, teachers, and technocratic economists, social workers, sociologists, physicians, and engineers*" (Rothbard, op. cit., p. 14). Instead of having of their behavior guided by priests, the gullible public now surrendered to the rule of the 'experts' as the new breed who claimed not to speak in the name of a God but as the disciples of 'science'.

Information was not yet free. Although it was no longer necessary to become a member of the clergy, but in order to gain access to knowledge, one had to pass the state-controlled school and university system. Against this mass of state-controlled information, the voices of liberty had no chance.

Antony P. Mueller

Death of the Gatekeepers

The printing press allowed the production and distribution of books and pamphlets and scientific treatises with much lower costs than before. This, in turn, encouraged literacy. But the process of literacy itself, in the form of public education, became a system of control. Access to knowledge has become wider, but it has remained restricted, manipulative, and concentrated. At the entrance to the access of knowledge stood the gatekeepers. Whether it be a school or a university, religious groups or political parties, the oligopolistic structure of power demanded control of the admittance to the realms of knowledge. It is no surprise, for example, that joining a political party is almost like joining a religious group. To climb the ranks of a political party is not much different from making a career in a religious order and both ways are not much different from an intellectual career. Gatekeepers are notorious in excluding unwanted truths and aborting new approaches that defy conventional wisdom.

Now, the ascent of the Internet marks the end of the gatekeepers. Prior to the information revolution, the predominance of oligopolistic structures was ubiquitous, as shown, for example, by the oligopoly of television stations. Now, with the Internet, the multitude of outlets encompasses all the media. The new ways of communication dissolve the old structures. One result of this revolutionary transformation is that informational constraint is over. Access and distribution of information are confronting few barriers as long as the basic liberties still prevail.

This new media revolution has a technical and a sociopolitical side. In the past, technology served as an instrument of exclusion, now it can serve as a means of inclusion. Times of transition are turbulent, and this is also the case with the new media. Much of what now seems dangerous, however, such as the apparent absence of informational filters and of a so-called quality control, will in the future appear as inconsequential as it is now with the Index of forbidden books of the past and the 'Imprimatur' of the Catholic Church.

The current informational revolution with the Internet at its center works in favor of freedom. Unlike in the past, when the media served specific groups to impose their will on the rest of society, the Internet revolution does the opposite. Instead of being instrumental for a limited group in their efforts of maintaining their rule, the Internet will challenge the concentration of power. In this sense, the current revolution is a libertarian revolution. Its first achievement is to dissolute power positions. This process is already in full swing.

Only still a few decades ago, it was costly to spread information. One needed a TV or radio station, for example, or had to launch a magazine or a newspaper. Nowadays, the Internet allows the world-wide storage and the dissemination of ideas at negligent costs. The old barriers are crumbling. Consequently, there is no longer a limitation on the variety of subjects to deal with. Before the information revolution, the providers - whether news channels, academic journals, or booksellers - were forced to focus their supply on the middle of the distribution curve to reach most customers. Because of limited space, the supply was restricted. Nowadays, with almost unlimited storage space, the offer extends to the long tails of the distribution.

With the Internet revolution, the costs of dissemination of new ideas have fallen close to zero. Likewise, access to information has become quasi costless. The consequence is an increase of the mass of information along with its diversification. This phenomenon ranges from music to academic texts. Mass and diversity are the hallmarks of the worldwide web. In the past, there has always been a trade-off between distribution and diversity. To maintain a tabloid with a wide circulation, for example, content had to focus on the most popular themes. Now, free of gatekeepers and with unlimited space, the special topics find a market.

In the past, power was concentrated in the hands of the gatekeepers. The guards decided what was 'correct' and what was 'false', what to publish and what not. The system of gatekeepers included the editors at TV stations and the newspapers, the referees of the scientific journals, and the decision-makers in the ministries of education along with all the other 'authorities' whose task was to take care of the 'truth' - which mostly was nothing but to hide the truths from the public because of the interests of power and because of prejudices.

Now, without the gatekeepers and with an almost limitless space available, diversity is spreading in the new media and it is up to the individual user to judge the content and to decide whether it is worth the access. In the past, the media gatekeepers practiced their power *ex officio* as an authoritarian activity. Claiming this role, the argument was to maintain 'quality standards', but this was a pretext given that the impediment was the limited space that made a screening indispensable. Different from an electronic platform of books, the brick and mortar library buildings have limited space. The modern media remove these restrictions and make the access time more flexible. The new world of information has become a world without major barriers where heterogeneity rules over homogeneity.

Antony P. Mueller

Toward the New World of Freedom

The oligopolistic era of modern history is ending. Dominance by the few is coming to an end. When barriers are low and almost nonexistent, supremacy is waning. Nevertheless, the old authorities still seek to maintain and regain their informational privileges. Yet when some governments turn off the Internet or limit access, they undermine their legitimacy and destroy the productivity of their economies. Governments that quit the global information network and shut-off their citizens will push their countries into an economic abyss and will fail to maintain their rule. Closed political systems are able to copy established technologies but have a hard time to develop new technologies.

At the same time when the barriers to the distribution of non-conformist information and opinions fall, the costs to maintain the established institutions are on the rise. Schools and universities, hospitals, and media outlets together with maintaining the welfare-warfare expenditures face an avalanche of costs that will ruin those states which try to go on as in the past. The state as we know it, will disappear. This way or the other: either by voluntary transformation or because of financial collapse. The question is whether the old order will go down with blood and tears or make peacefully way for a new liberty.

The foundations of the new information revolution are firm. Different from the past, this time the fundamentals promote freedom and diversification. The era of authentic liberalism has arrived. While in the past, the media favored authoritarian and totalitarian regimes because both the press and radio and television allowed hierarchical control, the global information network favors free access and distribution on a global scale. This constellation will limit and render the installation and maintenance of totalitarian regimes impossible. Implementing strict controls over the media is difficult. There are many chances that the new epoch in world history will become an era of libertarianism. Libertarianism as a political philosophy does not have, by its very nature, the goal of domination by exclusion as all other political ideologies have. Libertarianism promotes pluralism, diversification, and inclusion. In this sense, the new media, and the Internet are compatible with the libertarian political philosophy. This novelty represents a historical singularity.

Although the risks may seem small that a global totalitarian regime will emerge soon, one must take it into consideration and respond to it with strong voice case in favor of a libertarian revolution. Taking away power from the state is a moral necessity in the face of the prospect that the new technologies would put such an immense arsenal of surveillance and control into the hands of the state that a future totalitarian regime could exert complete control over the individual and produce the uttermost terror. Therefore, to establish an anarcho-capitalist order is a matter of human dignity.

What needs to be done as practical steps to establish a new order of liberty is, first, a change of the system of selection of the representatives through a lottery, called 'demarchy' or sortition.

Sortition (demarchy)

'Sortition' – also called 'demarchy' - is a form of governance that selects the representatives of the people as a random sample from a pool of candidates. Governance by selecting the people's representatives by lottery instead of elections can look back on a venerable history. For Aristotle (384 - 322 BC), to select the people's political representatives by lot instead of voting distinguishes the democracy from oligarchical rule: 'So it is ... democratic to occupy the offices by lot, and for the oligarchy by vote' (Aristotle, Politics, IV, 9, 1294b 7-9). Likewise, for Montesquieu (1689-1755) the lottery procedure corresponds to 'the nature of democracy' ('The spirit of the laws' - 1748).

In the ancient Greek polis, for the 'Great Council of the 500', as well as for judges and for some state officials, selection took place by the lot – as it is still partly the case in Switzerland. In the Republic of Venice, the selection procedure for the government and its members used the lottery in many ways. Until the 17th century, England also practiced the lottery system. Today, modern technology offers the possibility to apply random selection procedures to large populations.

The following advantages of demarchy are evident:
- High degree of popular legitimacy
- Independence of the representatives
- Absence of corruption
- No political parties
- Representation by normal people instead by political power seekers
- Elimination of the costs of the election campaigns
- Reduction of the overall cost of the political apparatus
- Comprehensible laws
- End of the inflation of laws, rules, and regulations
- Minimization of the state (less government spending, lower taxes).

Critics of demarchy claim that a parliament, whose members are selected by chance, has less expertise than an elected parliament, and that this would increase the power of the bureaucracy. The truth, however, is that the specific knowledge that is now present in the assemblies, exists in knowing how to gain and to exert power, and non-political competence is missing. Even more so, the current system of party politics has led to a huge bureaucracy and a massive build-up of the power of the state apparatus. The political parties and the bureaucratic apparatus cooperate to maximize their power which they achieve by having more state, not less.

***

The left-right scheme to denote one's position in the political spectrum is a dangerous device. Limiting the political spectrum to 'left' and 'right' deceives by its simplicity. It leaves a large area open in the center, at the top and at the bottom.

A better distinction than 'left' and 'right' is 'authoritarian' and 'libertarian'.

For the libertarian philosophy, self-ownership is a natural right. It implies the right to be free of aggression by others, including the state. For libertarians, 'freedom' does not mean that one could do as one likes but that each individual as a person owns himself and has a natural right to be free from aggression. Consequently, all legitimate social interaction must be voluntary. The social band that keeps the individuals together is reciprocity, be it in the form of economic exchange, or by friendship, love and sympathy.

The libertarian position is neither left nor right nor centrist. It goes beyond the 'liberal' and the 'conservative' creed as it opposes authoritarianism. Libertarianism also dismisses the distinction between personal and economic freedom because economic freedom is indispensable for personal freedom, and there is no economic freedom without personal freedom.

Sortition (demarchy) in the system of governance

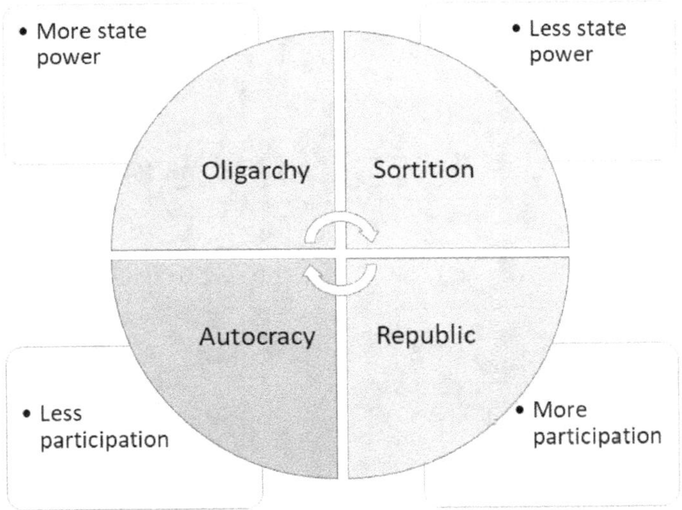

In this scheme, sortition in the upper right corner represents the highest degree of popular participation together with the lowest degree of state power.

In terms of degrees of participation of the people and the extent of state power, 'demarchy' is the system of governance, which represents the highest level of participation with the least state power (upper right segment).

A system of political party elections is an *oligarchy* and thus, although it allows limited popular participation, has a much higher extent of state power than sortition

Monarchy and *autocracy* have less participation than both oligarchy and sortition.

Autocracy has the least participation combined with the highest degree of state power.

Structure of governance

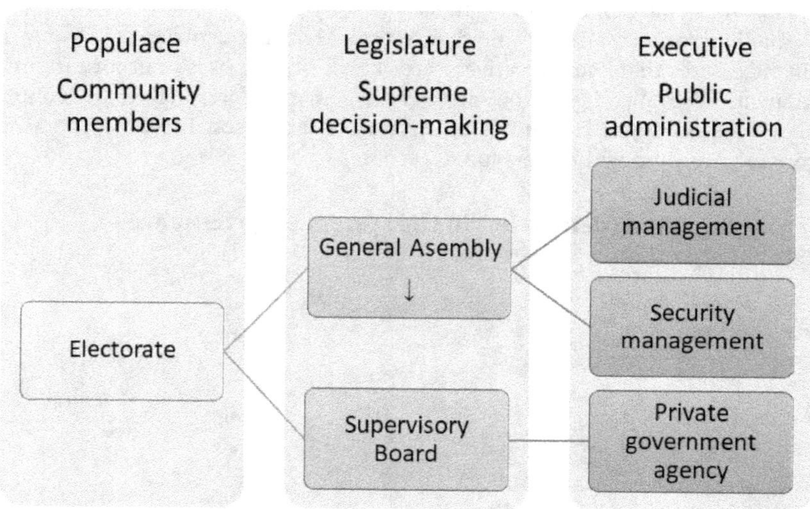

Agenda

The libertarian revolution is a soft revolution without violence. This is and will make the big difference between the anarcho-capitalist order and all other forms of governance. For the libertarian revolution to succeed, one must not 'take power', but conquer the public opinion by persuasion.

Steps on the path to demarchy

A.

Sortition for the Upper House (Senate) as a second chamber

Veto of the Upper House against additional public spending and against more taxes and regulations

Abolishment of the legal tender laws, freeze of the central bank money aggregate

B.

Transformation of the Upper House into the General Assembly

Constitution of the Supervisory Body

Private government management agencies for executive and judicial functions, policing, and defense

I.

Installation of a 'Senate chamber' with members selected by lot

II.

Senate exercises its veto power to halt state, politics, and bureaucracy

III.

Reform of the existing voting system. Establishment of a legislative body in the form of a General Assembly composed of representatives selected by lot

IV.

Reform of the state structure with the addition of a Supervisory Body and an Executive branch to the General Assembly

With the public support to change of the structure of the party democracy in place, the first step would be to complement the present system with an additional chamber. In this chamber - a kind of 'Senate' - members chosen by lot would possess veto rights over the decisions taken by the parliament (Congress) and government (presidency) including the judiciary (Supreme Court). Such a 'fourth power' is the 'voice of the people'. Although it is not yet a government and the lawgiver, the 'Senate' composed by members chosen by lot has the right to stop the encroachments of government and of the state bureaucracy because of the veto power it holds.

The next step would be to create a 'General Assembly' to serve as the prime law-giving body. The Assembly must be large enough to represent the people. For that purpose, it must comprise persons who are selected randomly among the constituency. Establishing the General Assembly requires a reform of the election laws. In order to achieve this, the libertarians must get a majority in the existing parliament (Congress). The final step in the reform of the state structure is to add a supervisory body and an executive branch of the Assembly.

The resulting institutional setting would include three organs: The General Assembly as the representative of the people and the prime law-giver, the Supervisory Body as a special committee to supervise the Executive branch that manages the current affairs of the polity.

The composition of the General Assembly results from a selection by lot according to the principle of 'one citizen one lot'. This legislative assembly must be large enough to provide a *representative sample* of the people. One-fourth of the Assembly should change on a rotating basis, every six months, so that each selected member will have a seat for twenty-four months. The General Assembly is the supreme body for promulgating the laws. It chooses among itself a Supervisory body who will select the government. The Supervisory body can invite, with the consent of the Assembly, qualified persons from outside to serve in the executive branch.

The composition of the General Assembly as the prime legislative body is the result of a random selection in line with the principle of universal suffrage. The General Assembly must be large enough to provide a representative sample of the constituency. Statistically, for example, a number of persons who fit into a large concert hall are adequate to represent a population from five million onwards to several hundred million at an acceptable margin of error and of high confidence, so that also populous countries could have a demarchy although the ideal would be small countries.

One-fourth of the Assembly change on a rotating basis every six month, so that each selected member will have a seat for two years. Every six months one fourth of the size of the Assembly enters while one-fourth leaves after having served for two years in the Assembly.

The Constituency as the body of citizens who have the right to participate in the sortition should be broad. One can leave it open to debate and to the individual situation of a country as to its size and heterogeneity - whether the members of the constituency are the same for general elections or should be more restrictive and only include those persons who register as candidates and who meet specific criteria. Because the demarchy also serves to select the representatives at the level of the individual states of a federation and for municipalities, there is ample room for experimentation with different schemes.

The General Assembly and the Executive

As the service in the General Assembly is for 24 months, each sixth months one-fourth of the members leave, while a new group of the same size enters as the new members of the Assembly. Before the entry of a new group, one fourth of the Assembly would have at this point have served 24 months, one fourth 18 months, one fourth 12 and one fourth and one more fourth would have served six months.

After each new selection, the Assembly exists of four groups with the new members having 24 months to serve, while the group that will leave has six more months to go. In terms of time served, the Assembly comprises four groups after a new selection, with the new group with zero months of service and the longest-serving group with 18 months of membership.

Rotation in Assembly

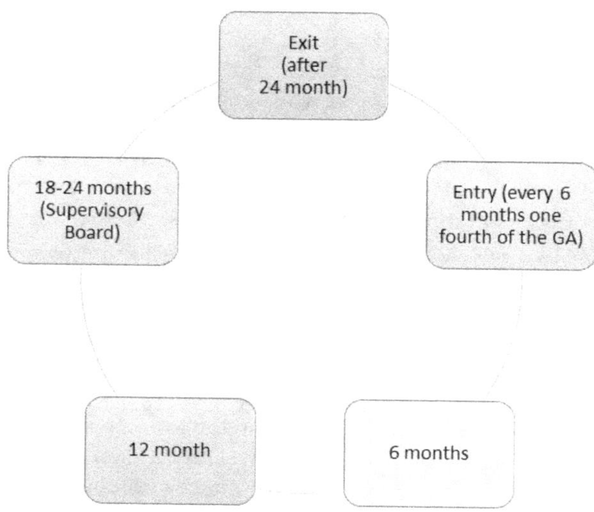

The General Assembly is the supreme body for promulgating the laws. It chooses among itself a Supervisory body that will nominate the government. The Supervisory body exists of the group of the longest-serving members of the General Assembly, that is the group which will leave in six months to return to civil life. The Supervisory body will hire, with the consent of the Assembly, qualified persons from outside to serve as the Executive.

The Supervisory body of the General Assembly oversees and controls the activities of the Executive. The Supervisory body hires a private government management firm to serve as the Executive. As it has been the case with private policing and arbitration, private government management companies will emerge under a libertarian order. These private government companies will offer their services first at the local community and municipal level from which the best firms will expand to the state and the level of unions of states.

Sortition structure

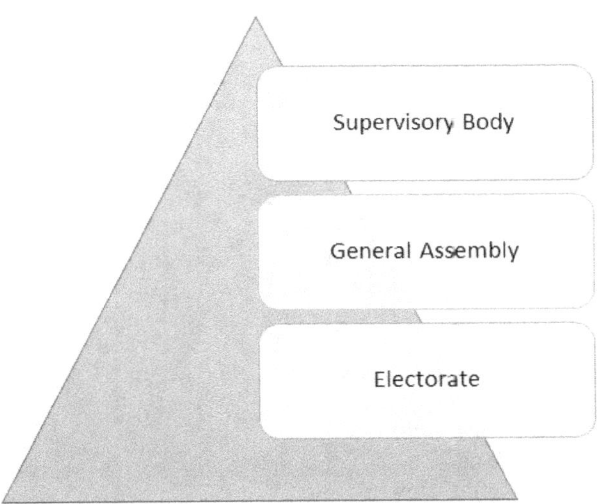

The personnel of these private government management firms will comprise professionals who, different from the governments of the past, will render their service under strict supervision of the Assembly. Private government management companies will employ full-fledged professionals. Their service will be cheaper and better than governments recruited from political parties. Additionally, much less of the personnel will be needed under privatization compared to the public services of nowadays - not only because the firms are private and thus more efficient but also because under a libertarian order the scope of state activities will drastically shrink. Law and order will be maintained at lower costs and with less encroachment on personal liberties.

When a community establishes a chamber, whose members are selected by lot as an addition to the existing structure of government, the 'Senate chamber' should use its veto right to stop all measures that would expand the state and its bureaucracy. After establishing the General Assembly as the prime law-giving body, intermediate measures must follow to reduce the state and its bureaucracy. In the long-run, the task to establish an anarcho-capitalist order requires to remove state money, to stop government spending and to eliminate all taxes and contributions along with eliminating public regulations and public employment, and to privatize the courts, the police force, and defense.

Timeline of the policies

Immediate Measures
- End expansion of money supply
- Stop expansion of government spending
- Halt rise of taxes and contributions
- Halt public regulations
- Stop hiring public employees

Intermediate Measures
- Open financial markets for free banking
- Reduce government spending
- Cut taxes and contributions
- Reduce regulations
- Diminish state employment

Long-term Measures
- Remove state money
- Eradicate government spending
- Eliminate taxes
- Minimize regulations
- Minimize public employment
- Privatize judicial courts
- Privatize police force
- Privatize defence
- Outsource government

Summary:
Why capitalism works, and socialism does not

Capitalism is a system in which profits come to those who are best at satisfying the wishes of the customers. 'Better' refers not only to the price but also to the quality, including the appeal of the product to the buyer. In a socialist economy, even a benevolent dictator could not provide the right mix of goods in terms of price and quality because in the socialist system, there are no market prices. Socialism eliminates both: information and incentives. All economic agents, including the planning authority, operate in the dark. A market economy, in contrast, functions like a data processing machine that emits the continuously information about scarcity and excess.

In a market economy, the relative prices of the goods serve as a guide for economic action. The price ratios show how to combine the production factors to best satisfy the needs of the consumers. Relative prices show what consumers want and guide the production process into this direction because this is where the profits emerge. The competition provides the incentives for cost-effectiveness so that consumers receive the goods at the lowest prices based on the best use of the factors of production.

In capitalism, the wishes of the clients regulate the overall structure of the price relations. The preferences of the consumers determine also the value of the investment goods. This so-called 'imputation' means that the value of the final product determines the value of the intermediate goods. Because the consumer determines the value of the final good, the anchor for the value structure of the entire wealth in a market economy is the consumer.

Under capitalism, it is not a planning authority that controls the production structure, but the consumers decide. Production follows the wishes of the consumers. They control the economy because only those entrepreneurs that obey the calls of their clients gain a profit. Businesses must restructure the production according to the changes of the wants, needs, and tastes of the buyers of their products.

Socialists suppose that to implant their rule on the economy all that is necessary is to socialize the private companies, replace the management, and install worker councils, and the new economic order would flourish. The early socialists expected that abundance would follow not least because now the workers would get what before went into the hands of the capitalists as profits. Yet the socialists ignored that the socialization of the means of production was just the beginning. They failed miserably in running the economy.

The planners may know what type of technology a specific production would require, and they can count on the professionalism of the engineers to use their knowledge. The error of socialist economic planning, however, is the to assume that business management could also continue as before after socialist operators take over the capitalist management. While the socialist regime can train administrators and engineers and put the party members in the position of directors, these new leaders cannot decide according to relative scarcities because there is no longer a private property-based entrepreneurial price system available.

Many supporters of socialism suppose that business management is nothing more than a kind of registration or simple bookkeeping. Vladimir Ilyich Lenin (1870–1924), the Soviet revolutionary leader, believed that the knowledge of reading and writing, and some expertise in the use of the four basic arithmetic operations and some training in accounting, would be enough for the conduct of business operations. The socialists then and now ignore the fundamental economic problem, which consists in determining what to produce, for whom, and how.

The socialist planners assume that a plan can stipulate these three tasks and ignore how and from where such a plan should find its standards of valuation. Socialists presume that one could manage a complex economy without capitalists and entrepreneurs. When prices and markets disappear, one loses the orientation about which factors of production are more and which are less scarce along with the loss of knowledge of the costs of the goods used in the production process.

Scarcity makes goods valuable, and relative prices show this in a market economy. By observing the prices, the market participants receive information about scarcity and align their economic decisions to the market signals. Yet when there is no market, information about the relation between the wants for goods and their supply vanishes. The price system informs about scarcity and abundance and makes it possible to decide according to one's own best interests. There is no need for a comprehensive system of information since markets enable to weigh the advantages and disadvantages of economic actions through relative prices because the price system reduces complexity for the individual decision maker to the single number of the price. In a market economy, the economic participants need only partial knowledge to act rationally.

In socialism, however, private ownership of the means of production no longer exists, and thus there is no price system for capital goods. Institutionally, socialism consists in abolishing the market economy and replacing it with a planned economy. Yet beyond the loss of private property, the fundamental problem comes from the consequence that by doing away with private property of the means of production, one wipes-out information. Even if the socialist administration puts price tags on the consumer goods, and the people may privately own consumer goods, there is no economic orientation about the relative scarcity of capital goods. Because the socialist system removes the private ownership of the production goods and eliminates the role of the entrepreneur, there are no markets.

The socialist economy does not serve the consumers. The point of reference for proper management is to execute the commands – the same as in the military. To fulfill plans refers to the respective level in the hierarchy of the command order – not to the consumer. Even if, for example, the central plan should stipulate to produce a certain number of a good, and that the order would go to the respective factories, the question arises how to design and by which combination of the factors of production the manufacturing should take place. Any production faces the problem that there is an almost unlimited number of ways how to produce a good. One can manufacture a commodity with very different raw materials, technologies, and combinations of the production factors and in an endless variety of designs.

Before one can systematically consider the aspects of the technological feasibilities, one must apply economic principles – the calculation of the potential profitability of producing a good. Without costs in relation to sales, a technical evaluation makes no sense. What is technically possible is not economically recommended, and what appears efficient from a technical point of view need not be so in terms of economic expediency. With costs left out of the consideration, socialist production is blind to the risk of producing goods that would cost more than they are worth.

Who determines value? In a market economy, it is the client, and, in the last instance, the consumer. In central planning economy, it is up to the planners to determine the value. This, however, they cannot accomplish because preferences and technologies change, and the complexity of the relationship among the goods exceeds the capacity of anyone's mind or that of a planning committee to grasp.

Socialism suffers from four fundamental defects. Each one of them alone makes socialism already inoperative. Together they multiply the effect.

First, socialism eradicates private property and markets and thus eliminates rational calculation.

Second, socialism allows soft budgets, so there is no mechanism in place to discards inefficient production methods.

Third, abolishing private property and replacing it by the state promotes distorted incentives.

Fourth, the socialist system with its absence of private property and of free markets inhibits economic coordination of the system of division of labor and capital.

Socialism means economic blindness. Information gets lost along with the incentive to act according to the price signals. In capitalism, the motivations of gaining profits and to avoid costs work as an incentive to behave rationally. In a market economy, the prices fulfill the double function to inform and to incentivize the seller and the buyer.

It is no wonder that even a degenerate capitalism produces more prosperity than the best socialism. Therefore, the task ahead cannot be to remove capitalism in favor of socialism but to make capitalism better which means to make it more capitalist.

Outlook

While the 20th century experienced the profound transformation of manufacturing, technology is now revolutionizing the service sector. The professionals - ranging from medical doctors to lawyers, from educators to public administrators - will face tough challenges. The transformation is already on its way. Many apparently secure jobs will be wiped out. Robots and artificial intelligence make complex tasks not only cheaper but also perform better. The new technologies enter the consultants' offices, the legal chambers, the classrooms, and the hospitals. With a click, better diagnoses than humans could deliver show up on the screen in seconds - be it a medical assessment or the analysis of a legal problem. Machines are replacing even sophisticated occupations. What does the future hold for jobs, skills, and wages? What does this mean for the future of capitalism? What kind of economic system is best to meet the challenge?

In the 19th century, one could tell the farm boy to go to the city and learn a trade. In the 20th century, one could say to the young man or girl they should move ahead and go to study. These were all good pieces of advice. Yet in the new millennium, there is nowhere to go upward. The move from agriculture to industry, and from industry to the services, has ended. Now, to go to the university and to get a degree is no longer a guarantee for a well-paid and secure job. Professional positions fall victim to automatization and to the onslaught of artificial intelligence. The sprouts of the ladder are occupied. For one to go up, another one must come down. Upwardly mobile is a feat of the past.

What is the way out? The promise of 'jobs, jobs, jobs' will be in vain. The more the state tries to make jobs available and positions more secure, the more productivity declines, and incomes fall. The new millennium needs a different approach. The answer is to fully embrace technology. The more the new technologies become a complement to human work, productivity will rise. The urgency of having a fixed position as an employed person recedes. The use of one's car as a chauffeur for and renting out one's house or apartment for travelers with are examples of the things to come.

A necessary condition for the surge in productivity is less state and the end of politics. Less state and fewer politics would deliver the citizen from the heavy burden that now confronts him. Productivity would rise as the state fades away. The individual gets liberated from both sides. On the one hand, the burden of taxes and contributions falls. On the other hand, gains of productivity bring down the costs of living.

The current 'all-or-nothing'-trap ('either Yale or jail') would vanish. Now it is so that if one has a professional job, one's material situation is fine. Yet when one loses this position, the fall is enormous. We need a system that avoids this dichotomy. An anarcho-capitalist order would bring down the burden of taxes and of contributions. Free capitalism would open the path to vast productivity gains. Then, the urgency of having a permanent earning position would recede. One could live well even without having a secure job because productivity is so high that also temporary assignments offer a pay that is high enough to maintain a good life. The technology that takes away the jobs is the same that provides the tools which brings down the costs of living and makes leisure time attractive.

Nowadays, there are many professional couples who are both working because one needs two incomes to do well. Many would be glad to have only one breadwinner if they could maintain their living standard. Free capitalism would offer such chances because taxes and contributions would come down to a tenth of the present level and goods would cost less than half of their present prices with income several times higher than today.

Our present economic, political, and judicial system is ill-prepared for the challenge of the future. That was also the case over a hundred years ago at the beginning of the 20th century. Then, many wrong decisions were taken until a system took shape and became accepted that could accommodate the technological changes and the economic transformations. Yet now, new tribulations loom, and they make the dominant 'liberal' - social-democratic - system obsolete.

Resistance will arise - like that which came from the artisans and the home workers at the start of the industrial revolution. The workers feared that with introducing the new machines they would lose their economic existence and be condemned to poverty and misery. Yet they had no chance. And good for them - for because of the industrial revolution, the working class experienced a level of prosperity in the two centuries to come which was unimaginable at the time when the industrial revolution took off.

Protectionism, interventionism, imperialism, communism, and fascism were the many wrong answers in the past. Many believe now that the social-democratic version of capitalism would be the adequate system for the new millennium. Yet this not the case. It is no exaggeration to forecast that when we continue with the social-democratic way, the end would be state-bankruptcy. Serious analyses must conclude that the social security and welfare complex of healthcare, education, pensions, and social assistance have failed. The legal system is in shambles. Likewise, the expectation that the political management of the economy could guarantee employment, economic growth, and financial stability, is illusionary. Trying to maintain, to reform, and to expand the present system will lead to the opposite of the 'liberal' promises.

Without a change of the social security system, healthcare costs alone will absorb more than one fourth of the gross incomes. Pension provisions would require another fourth of the income. In a few decades, the ordinary taxpayer must confront obligatory contributions that exceed half of the income to pay for social security and welfare alone. Besides these contributions, the government would have to require another third of the incomes as taxes to finance defense and the other parts of the state apparatus. Such a burden is impossible to bear. Almost nothing would be left for private use. Before these projections can become a reality, the economy would break down. People would refuse to work, and businesses would stop to invest, the nation would become bankrupt.

Thus, the challenge remains: in the decades to come, young people can no more expect to have a high income just because they get a university diploma. Many job-secure careers in established professions will go away or experience profound transformations. The present horror of unemployment or of not finding the right job comes from being not able to bear the high costs of education, healthcare, housing, public security, and retirement without a high permanent income.

We need a new order. Repairs of the structures in place are not enough. Just as it had made no sense to improve the horse carriage to compete with the automobile, is it a futile effort to improve the current political system and to make the social security system more effective and the economy more efficient.

We need to make a turnaround. Instead of making the present system more social-democratic, we need a libertarian revolution. Instead of making capitalism more socialist, we need a more capitalist capitalism.

A free economy in a free society requires three major institutional changes.

First, the selection of the society's representative body through a process of random selection;

second, a private monetary system to substitute the central banks;

third, the provision of law and security by private suppliers.

In order to establish a state-free society, insight must come first. The legitimacy of a free social order cannot come from the application of force - as it has been the case with all other political systems - but needs as its base the voluntary cooperation of the people to arise as a spontaneous order.

The tentative to establish an 'improved socialism', as it is the aim of the globalist scheme of a world government, would be even more deadly than the socialism of the 20th century. Yet also the milder forms of socialism and fascism, as they are practiced as interventionism, represent no valuable alternative. Likewise, it is pointless to expect that government could manage the economy and provide stability and economic growth so that everybody could have a well-paid secure job.

What we need is a new political and economic order, an order, which does not dilute capitalism with socialism, but a capitalism free of its socialist admixtures. The more the state would retreat from private life, the less the burden of taxes would become. The present schemes of healthcare, education, pensions, legal services, housing, and welfare - not to speak of defense - are not only inefficient but also costly beyond needs. In these areas, the new technologies provide ample alternatives that would lower the costs while making the services better. Doing away with politics would eliminate the silly election campaigns. Sortition would stop the political culture of more government spending.

If we go on with the present system, the state will grow bigger and bigger. With the growing size of the state, governments will become more powerful. Without a halt, the present so-called 'liberal democracy' will transmute into a new totalitarianism.

The great debate is not only about jobs, but even more so how we can maintain human freedom in the face of the new technologies. In the new millennium, the demise of the state is a necessary condition for freedom. If we fail, humanity's fate is an age of slavery. If we succeed, we may welcome a new era of freedom and prosperity. Full employment is a dream of the past. Likewise, it is an empty hope that government could do anything about it. Guaranteed employment would only repeat the errors of socialism. Interventionism and macroeconomic management that should provide employment, growth, and financial stability, do no longer work. Even worse: the more assignments, responsibilities, and rights we assign to the government, the more totalitarian the state will become. With the modern technology at hand, the state of the new millennium would gain all the tools it takes to establish a regime of comprehensive repression with not a trace left of human freedom and dignity.

The hope for the new epoch is not less but more capitalism. The more complex society and the economy have become, the more one needs markets as the instrument of coordination and private initiative.

Free capitalism provides the essentials for prosperity and freedom: efficient coordination of individual plans based on voluntary exchange and high productivity.

The coming decades will experience a profound transformation in areas such as law, medicine, education, and public administration - those fields of activity where many of university-educated professionals have found stable and well-paid positions. In the decades to come more of the jobs that seem as secure will disappear or undergo drastic transformations. It is futile to expect that a college degree would be enough to guarantee a well-paid and stable position. A great wave of substitution of machines for labor, which occurred in the 19th century in agriculture, and in the 20th century in manufacturing, will take now place in the service sector including the high-level services.

The current system of managed capitalism is incapable to cope with the challenges of the new era. Not more government is the solution but higher productivity, and to achieve higher productivity we need less state and fewer politics.

To meet the challenge of precarious employment, a drastic reduction in the costs of living will help. This goal requires productivity, and only free capitalism can generate the economic efficiency. We must embrace technological progress in all its forms because this is how productivity will increase. Productivity is not the problem, it is the solution. The problem is the cost of the state and the detrimental effects of the governmental activity.

Along with the concerns of how to get jobs, an even darker danger is lurking. If we do not abolish the state and politics in time, the new technologies will become horrendous instruments of totalitarian control in the hands of the governments. The larger the state and the more powerful the government, the bigger the threat. We must diminish the power of the state and reduce politics to regain and maintain our freedom.

Minimizing and doing away with the state is an urgent mission because otherwise, the modern technology would put terrific instruments of control into the hands of the government. With the new technical devices of supervision and domination, a modern totalitarian state could supersede the terror and suppression of anything in history. The state is not only superfluous and a danger for human liberty but has become a threat to human existence.

Society is a system of coordination. Coordination can be vertical or horizontal: either as a hierarchy of commandos and violent sanctions or voluntary exchange and cooperation. Of all known procedures of coordination, markets work best. There is no other system of production beyond free capitalism that could match pure capitalism's high productivity.

The current political system is not a democracy but is party politics; the economy is not a free market economy but suffers from intervention and state management. To be free and prosperous, this must change.

As the book details, we need a radical reduction of the state and its bureaucracy. The share of the state of around fifty percent of overall production is too high. Public debt is growing and moving the nation toward bankruptcy. The people must bear immense burdens in taxes and contributions. To solve the dilemma, the costs of living must fall. This goal requires productivity, and only free capitalism can generate the economic efficiency.

The point is not having more jobs but to have a system where one need not worry about jobs because the urgency to have one is not so great as it is now. With the massive burden of costs now in place, having a well-paid and stable position is a necessity for gaining a good life. Under a free capitalism, this would change. Productivity would be so high that the costs of living would be low. There will be top jobs available which pay well, but those with a precarious employment situation need not worry because they can also have a good life – including entertainment, which due to the new technologies comes almost for free. Drastic cost reductions would occur in medicine, education, and public administration. Other big cost items, such as transports, would likewise fall in price. Most of all, with the state and politics gone or at least reduced to a minimum, the menace of a suppressive state terror will dissipate.

The organization of politics as a system of competing political parties is an obstacle on the way to the new system. Modern democracy is party politics. Candidates win by false promises. The state expands without delivering better services.

Sortition, the selection of the people's representative by lot, would do away with the wasteful and harmful system of party politics. Choosing the legislative body not by vote but by chance would usher into a new era and mark the move away from oligarchical rule and to an authentic democracy.

Together with privatizing money and of the legal system, ending party politics would open the path to a more prosperous economy with high productivity. There would be no public debt. The burden of contributions and taxes would sink.

With the cost of living down, the risk of unemployment loses its menace.

Under an anarcho-capitalist order, temporary or even prolonged unemployment would not be a castigation as it is now. What capitalism is all about is to substitute capital for human labor and to liberate us from the burden of tedious work and from the worries about our next meal and where to lay our head at night.

In order to win the public opinion, libertarianism must present itself as a forward-facing movement whose origins are the rebellions against authoritarianism, dictatorship, and totalitarianism. Libertarians must denounce socialism as old-fashioned, stagnant, and backward-looking. Libertarians must ridicule socialism as the superstition of the modern age. Libertarianism is neither a conservative movement nor is it libertine. The enemy of libertarianism is power. The goal of libertarianism is liberty and its means are peaceful.

Libertarianism as governance and as an anarcho-capitalist economic order stands in the finest intellectual tradition and as such, has been the spearhead of the best that modern age has to offer. Libertarianism represents those elements of modernity that are sound, solid, and ethical. Libertarians must convince public opinion that anarcho-capitalism is a system of governance of the highest standards of intellectual standing and ethics. Anarcho-capitalism is the path to both liberty and prosperity.

The promoters of anarcho-capitalism must nourish the prospect that an anarcho-capitalist order will be a world of plenty. Libertarians must convince the public that under an anarcho-capitalist order, net salaries would rise, first, because there would be much less taxes and contributions to pay and, second, because of the increase in productivity. Beyond that, the purchasing of money would rise because of falling prices. Under an anarcho-capitalist economy, a many-fold increase of wide-spread wealth will happen - and this would only be the beginning.

Anarcho-capitalists must propagate the insight that to produce the so-called public goods is not only inefficient but also useless. Besides being expensive, much of the state-run education and medicine is not only superfluous but prejudicial. The military is needed not because people are bad but because there are states run by psychopaths.

Without taking the power out of the hands of the professional politicians, libertarianism has no chance to become a reality. Therefore, demarchy is a necessary step towards an anarcho-capitalist order. For this to happen, a change of the prevalent ideology must take place. Libertarians must transform public opinion in favor of sortition, the selection of the people's representatives by the lot. For this purpose, the libertarians must refer to the vast number of examples of current and historical examples of the foolishness, idiocy, and brutality of a leadership, which is selected by force and vote. The viciousness, ruthlessness, cruelty, and vindictiveness of these rulers stands in sharp contrast to what leadership under demarchy would be. Most people will see that when normal people are the rulers, the horrors that have come with the political leadership that has come to power by force and vote is a thing of the past. Along with the research and documentation of the past and present behavior of the professional politicians, libertarians should support and extend all forms of ridicule to shed upon the electoral political processes.

As to the theory, advocates of the anarcho-capitalist economic model should not so much stress their allegiance to its historical roots but emphasize that their practitioners march in the frontline of theoretical progress.

Entrepreneurs must abandon their alliance with the state as they have practiced it in the age of corporate capitalism. The state is a mean partner. In the future, besides being malicious, the state will become impotent because of the lack of funds. Reliance on the state is a lost issue. Under state capitalism, individual companies gain special advantages with the help from the state at the cost of the business community. This is not only unethical, but also uneconomical. Businessmen must form a new alliance. Their rightful partner is not the state but the libertarian movement. Instead of throwing money into the mouths of corrupt politicians, the business community would do well for its own future and the prosperity of all if they would fund the libertarian movement.

A wide and fecund field of intellectual projects calls for the endeavors not only of economists and jurists, but also of libertarian historians, political scientists, and sociologists and of the other disciplines, including theology and psychology. Research in these areas needs a new focus: no longer as the praise of the state and of its leaders but, on the contrary, reveal the failure of the state and its leaders.

In this great effort to create a better world and to save humankind from tyranny, everyone has a role to play. The work must begin now because a long way lies ahead of us.

III.

CONCEPTS AND PRINCIPLES

> *"A man who chooses between drinking a glass of milk and a glass of a solution of potassium cyanide does not choose between two beverages; he chooses between life and death. A society that chooses between capitalism and socialism does not choose between two social systems; it chooses between social cooperation and the disintegration of society. Socialism is not an alternative to capitalism; it is an alternative to any system under which men can live as human beings."*
> Ludwig von Mises: Human Action (Scholar's Edition 1998), p. 676

Socialism-Capitalism
Concepts of Demarchy
Anarcho-individualist order - basic concepts
Main types of government failures
Ten fundamental indictments against the State
Principles of economic governance
Principles of anarcho-capitalism
Principles of anarchist individualism

If we go on with the present system, the state will grow bigger and bigger. With the growing size of the state, governments will become more powerful.

Under a socialist state, the new technologies of surveillance and control would become horrific instruments.

In the new millennium, the demise of the state is a necessary condition for freedom. If we fail, humanity's fate is an age of slavery. If we succeed in establishing an anarcho-capitalist order, we may welcome a new era of freedom and prosperity.

A free economy in a free society requires three major institutional changes.

First, the selection of the society's representative body through a process of random selection, called demarchy (sortition);

second, a private monetary system to substitute the central banks;

third, the provision of government, law enforcement, and security by private suppliers.

SOCIALISM – CAPITALISM

When discussing socialism, the first thing to do is distinguish between 'socialism as a goal' and 'socialism as a method'. Without this difference, one gets easily deceived and, indeed, many people are fooled into believing that to achieve the socialist goal of prosperity for all one must install socialism as a means. By implanting socialism as a method, the opposite of the expected prosperity comes. Instead of prosperity for all, misery and the loss of freedom is the result. The socialist trick their believers into the illusion that because socialism as a goal is so good, socialism as a means is the right way to obtain this goal.

The concept of socialism entails the contradiction between goal and method.

The concept of capitalism does not suffer from this confusion. Capitalism is a means. The goal of capitalism is the production of prosperity, not much different from the socialist ideal, yet be very different means. There are two fundamental ways of capitalism as a means: one is state capitalism, where capitalism is embedded in a state and under the control of government, and the other way is free or anarcho-capitalism where voluntary exchange relations rule.

Socialism's contradiction between method and goal

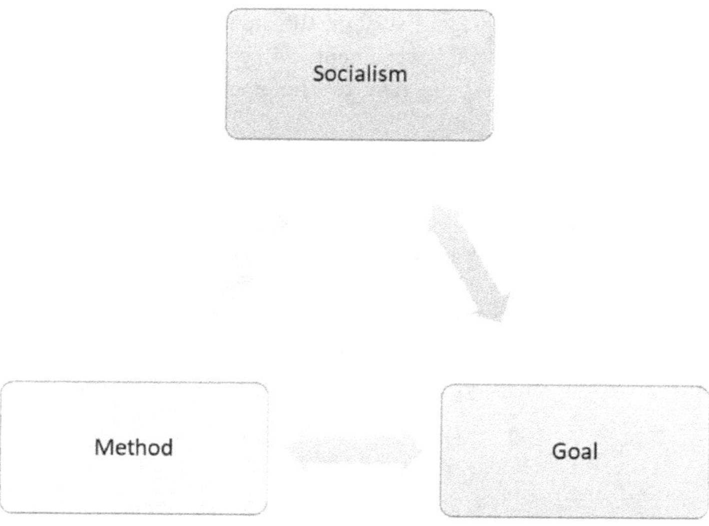

The dispute about capitalism and socialism does not concern the goals, but the means. Which is better to achieve prosperity and freedom? When one puts the problem this way, the answer becomes obvious. Theoretically and historically, socialism has failed on all counts. Therefore, the problem is not socialism versus capitalism, because only fools or fully misguided people would choose socialism. The question is which kind of capitalism is the better method to produce prosperity for all: state capitalism or anarcho-capitalism?

In the past, various forms of state capitalism emerged, most prominently the social market economy since the inception of the second half of the 20th century. The case for anarcho-capitalism comes from the need of doing away with the deficiencies of the present system, which, due to a democracy based on political parties, has produced an excess of government spending which has slowed down economic progress and where the welfare state has not lessened but increased inequality.

Capitalism – methods and goal

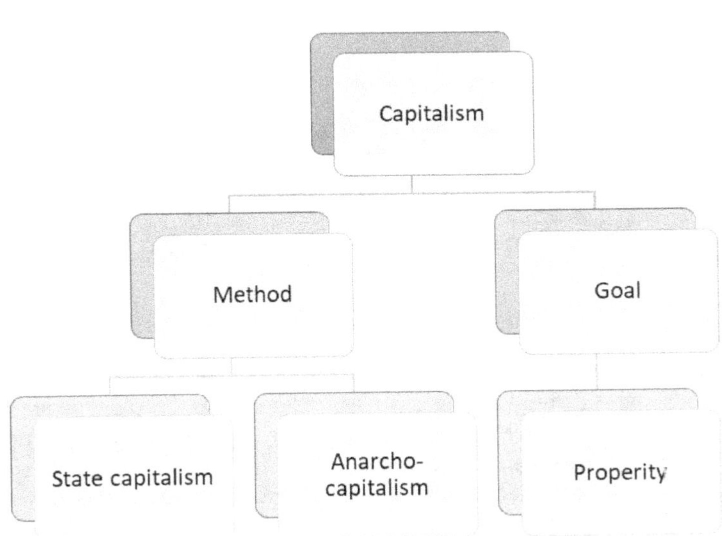

Anarcho-capitalism and electoral democracy are incompatible. To give anarcho-capitalism a chance, the political system must change. The way out of dilemma is demarchy or sortition, a political system where the representatives of the people are selected not by vote but by chance. The polity of a free republic consists in the combination of anarcho-capitalism, demarchy, and private government management.

What is the advantage of anarcho-capitalism over state capitalism? The answer is that anarcho-capitalism generates higher levels of productivity, and that productivity is the source of wealth. Demarchy is necessary to do away with the competition of political parties whose rivalry leads to the appropriation of the state as an instrument of distribution. Private government management is an agency that exerts governmental functions as executive and judicial body without the dominance that comes with the state functions. A free republic must be a polity beyond the state and politics.

Polity of a Free Republic

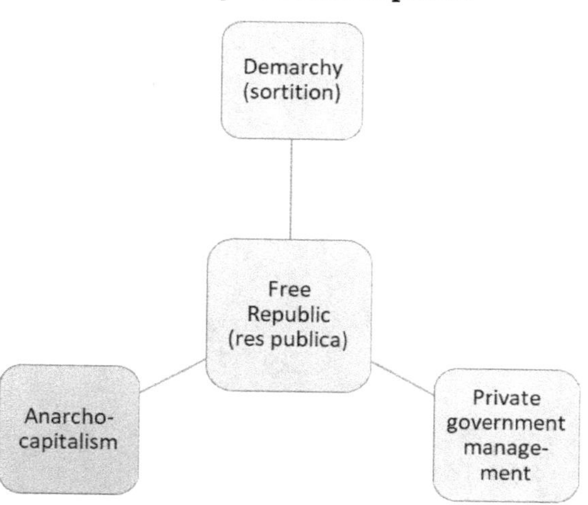

The socialists presume that under a socialist regime the rate of technological progress would be the same as under capitalism. They claim that with the removal of the profit motive one could improve working conditions and have an equal distribution of income. Yet the socialists do not see that the profit motive is the main factor of stimulating technological progress. In a market economy, business can obtain a higher profit rate by way of better productivity, and a higher productivity requires technological progress.

Historically, the evidence shows that technological progress has come with capitalism, and capitalism has come with free enterprise.

The socialists also discard the role of capital and of personal freedom. The socialists see only the accumulated capital but disregard capital accumulation and capital maintenance, i.e. saving. Socialist see the capitalist as an exploiter when in fact his main function if the provision of savings. Likewise, technological progress will not occur in a society where there is no freedom of speech and of private initiative. The meta factors of a capitalist economy are capital accumulation (saving), private initiative (personal freedom) and profit orientation.

Meta factors of a capitalist economy

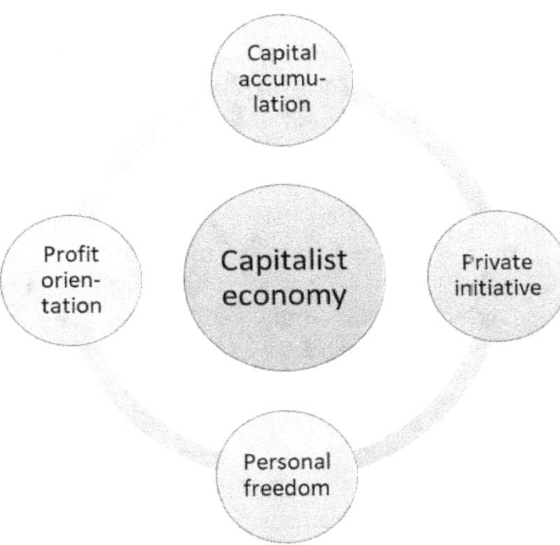

Antony P. Mueller

Concepts of Demarchy

The present system of state capitalism has become an obstacle to wealth creation. Under the political system of the modern party-democracy, there is a constant pressure at work to expand government. The rule of the party democracy undermines the free market economy. Interventionism and taxation have become the trademark of the modern State. In order to bring the economy back on the path to prosperity, a fundamental change must be made: not only with the economic order but also with government. Even more, the breakthrough must also encompass the spiritual attitude. The triumph of free capitalism comes with the self-liberation of the individual. Anarcho-capitalism and anarcho-individualism are the two sides of the same coin of a free republic.

The present order is under the full authority of the State. While classical liberalism could still make a distinction between family, society, nation, and state, these distinctions have disappeared in the modern State which has become totalitarian not only in its fascist or socialist shaping. The modern State in its current form as a democracy appears only gentle in its appearance. Behind this façade, this State is as brutal and as violent as any of its predecessors. The modern State has become all-encompassing and subsumes under its authority the nation, government, and the people.

Total State

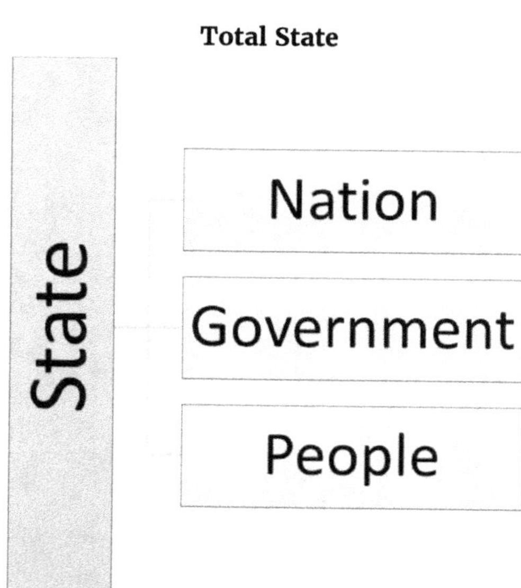

In order to distinguish the present State from a polity of free men, an appropriate term seems to be 'anarcho-republicanism'. Anarcho-republicanism is a polity whose constituent elements are personal ownership, private property, voluntary association, and non-aggression.

Anarcho-republicanism defines a polity based on the voluntary association of free persons for the cooperative attainment of individual aims, a polity that is a republic ("res publica") in its true sense different from state organizations that are hierarchical, dictatorial, and authoritarian.

As to its governance, the anarcho-republic requires an order whose authority is not the State but the people as the term "republic" in the sense of "res publica" - public matters - denotes.

Rule of the res publica

The structure of such a *polity* would comprise a General Assembly composed of members chosen by lot, a Supervisory Board as a special committee as part of the General Assembly and the government, which exerts the executive functions as a private management company under the authority of the General Assembly and the Supervisory Board.

Republic

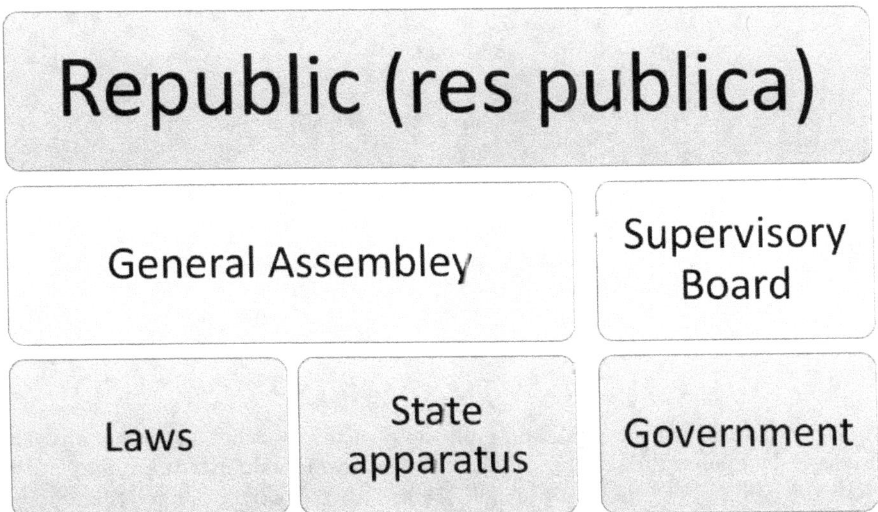

While anarcho-individualism denotes the philosophy, libertarianism stands for the political movement aimed at establishing the governance of free persons. Libertarianism stands against all those movements which try to establish an authoritarian or a dictatorial rule. Anarcho-liberalism is the specific political philosophy which promotes a polity based on the voluntary association of free persons for the cooperative attainment of individual aims.

"Demarchy" is a form of governance where the people's representatives are chosen by lottery in contrast to the political systems whose rulers come to power through heritage, force or vote, while "sortition" designates the process through which the representative body of the people is chosen in a lottery in contrast to systems of vote, co-option, and cooptation. Those selected by lot form the members of the General Assembly, which is the representative body of the electorate that form the legislative body of the Republican Polity similar to parliaments or congresses in the modern democracies.

Institutional structure of a Demarchy

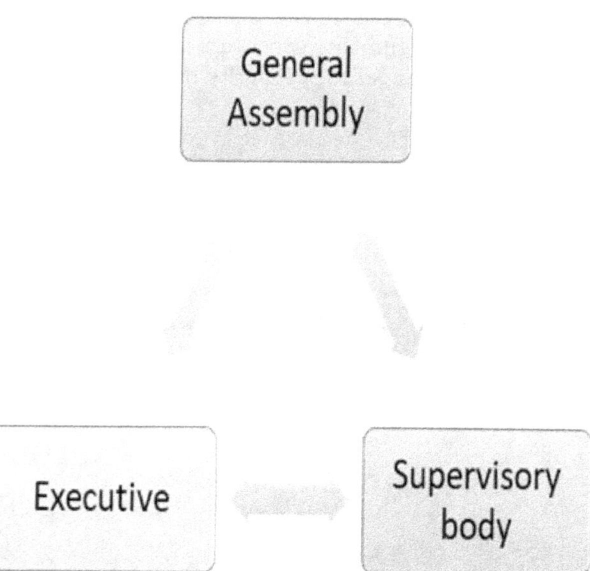

Anarcho-individualism is the guiding philosophy of the model of a free republic. The anarcho-individualist philosophy puts the sovereign individual at the center of the system of values in contrast to all forms of collectivism and hierarchical authoritarian organizations.

The supervisory body is a part of the General Assembly with special assignments of supervision over the private government management agency resembling the old

Upper House in Britain or Senates in the original meaning.

In the polity of a free republic, the government is a private government agency that is hired by the General Assembly and supervised by the Supervisory Body to exert executive functions akin to governments in the traditional sense yet without state authority. The judicial management is done by private law agencies that offer services of arbitration similar to current arbitration services and private law agencies that offer services of arbitration similar to current arbitration services. Likewise, policing is assigned to Private police similar to the present forms of non-state law-enforcement bodies. The defense is under the authority of the General Assembly and of the supervision by the Supervisory body, the defense of the community is managed by private companies.

Anarchistic Individualism

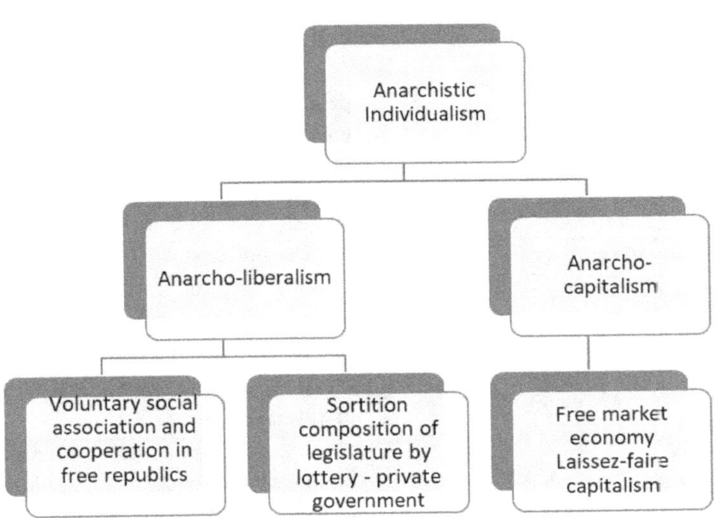

In the context of the polity of a free republic, anarcho-capitalism refers to a free market economy ("Laissez-faire"-capitalism) - an economic order based on private property and free markets in contrast to state capitalism, socialism, communism, and interventionism.

ANARCHO-INDIVIDUALIST ORDER
BASIC CONCEPTS

Concept	Definition
Anarcho-republic	A polity based on the voluntary association of free persons for the cooperative attainment of individual aims, a polity that is a republic ("res publica") in its true sense different from state organizations that are hierarchical, dictatorial, and authoritarian
Anarcho-liberalism	The political philosophy which promotes a polity based on the voluntary association of free persons for the cooperative attainment of individual aims
Libertarianism	The political movement aimed at establishing the governance of free persons. Libertarianism stands in contrast to all those movements which try to establish an authoritarian or dictatorial rule
Demarchy	A form of governance where the people's representatives are chosen by lottery in contrast to the political systems whose rulers come to power through heritage, force or vote
Sortition	The process through which the representative body of the people is chosen in a lottery in contrast to systems of vote, co-option, and cooptation
Anarcho-capitalism	Free market economy ("Laissez-faire"-capitalism) - an economic order based on private property and free

	markets in contrast to state capitalism, socialism, communism, and interventionism
Anarcho-individualism	The philosophy that puts the autonomous individual at the center of the system of values in contrast to all forms of collectivism and hierarchical authoritarian organizations
Electorate	Members of the community that form the universe of the sortition similar to the voters in a democracy
General Assembly	The representative body of the electorate that form the legislative body of the Republican Polity similar to parliaments or congresses in the modern democracies
Supervisory Body	A part of the General Assembly with special assignments of supervision over the private government management agency similar to the old Upper House in Britain or Senates in the original meaning
Government management	A private government agency that is hired by the General Assembly and supervised by the Supervisory Body to exert executive functions similar to governments in the traditional sense yet without state authority
Judicial management	Private law agencies that offer services of arbitration similar to current arbitration services
Policing	Private police similar to the present forms of non-state law-enforcement bodies
Defense	Under the authority of the General Assembly and of the supervision by the Supervisory body, the defense of the community is managed by private

	companies (high-tech)

MAIN TYPES OF GOVERNMENT FAILURES

I.

Knowledge

Government policies suffer from the pretense of knowledge (Friedrich Hayek). In order to perform a successful market intervention, politicians need to know much more than they possibly can. Market knowledge is not centralized, systematic, organized and general, but dispersed, heterogeneous, specific, and individual. Different from a market economy where there are many operators and a constant process of trial and error, the correction of government errors is very limited because of its status as a monopoly and because admitting errors may actually be worse for the reputation of the politician than sticking with a wrong decision - even against one's own insight.

II.

Information asymmetries

While there are also information asymmetries' in the market, for example between the insurer and the insured, or between the seller of a used car and its buyer, the information asymmetry is more profound in the public than in the private sector. While there are, for example, several insurance companies and many car dealers, there is only one government. The representatives of the state as an agency, the politicians, have no skin the game and because they are no stakeholders, they will not make much efforts to investigate and avoid information asymmetries'. On the contrary, politicians are typically eager to provide funds not to those who need them most but to those who are politically most relevant.

III.

Crowding out of the private sector

Government intervention does not eliminate apparent market deficiencies but creates them by crowding out the private supply. If there were not a public dominance in the areas of schooling and social assistance, private supply and private charity would fill the gap as it was the case before government usurped these activities. Crowding-out of the private sector through government policies is constantly at work because politicians can get votes by offering additional public services although the public administration would not improve but rather deteriorate the issue.

IV.

Time lags

Government policies suffer from long lags between diagnoses and effect. Government notices only those problems for which there is a political pressure. It takes a long time until a problem becomes sufficiently politicized until it finds the attention of the government. After the diagnosis, another lag happens until the authorities have found a consensus on how to tackle the political problem and it takes a further time span until the appropriate political means have found sufficient political support. Only then will the measures get implemented and a further time elapses until the proceedings show some effects. The results of state interventions typically not only deviate from the original intent but actually may produce the opposite result. In every case, the lapse of time between the articulation of a problem and effect is so long that not only the nature of the problem and its context have changed - often fundamentally.

V.

Rent seeking and rent creation

Government intervention invites rent-seeking. Rent seeking is the endeavor of gaining privileges through government policies. Along with existing rents, government policies are induced to create additional rent opportunities in order to gain additional support and votes. This rent creation invites more rent-seeking and leads to a process where the distinction between corruption and decent and legal conduct get blurred. The more a government gives in to rent-seeking and rent creation, the more the country will fall victim to clientelism, corruption, and the misallocation of resources.

VI.

Logrolling and vote trading

The public choice concept of "logrolling" denotes the exchange of favors among the political factions in order to get one's favored project through by supporting the projects of the other group. This conduct leads to the steady expansion of state activity. Through the "quid pro quo," the politicians support pieces of legislation of other factions in exchange for obtaining the political support for one's own piece of legislation. This comportment leads to the well-known phenomenon of "legislative inflation", the avalanche of useless, contradictory and detrimental law production.

VII.

Common good

The so-called "common good" is not a well-defined concept. Similar concepts, such as that of the "public good" which is defined by non-excludability and non-rivalry, misses the point because it is not the good that is "common" or "public" but its provision is deemed as more effective by collective efforts than individuality. However, this is the case with all goods and the market itself is a system of providing private goods through cooperative efforts. Any of the so-called public goods, which the government supplies, the private sector can also deliver, and cheaper and better. A free market economy could not only provide education, health care or old age provision as well as domestic and external security but also better and cheaper.

VIII.   Regulatory capture
The term "regulatory capture" denotes a government failure where the regulatory agency does not pursue the original intent of promoting the "public interest" but fall victim to the special interest of those groups, which the agency was set up to regulate. The capture of the regulatory body by private interests means that the agency turns into an instrument to advance the specific interest of the groups that were targeted for regulation. The special interest group may ask for regulation to obtain the state apparatus as the instrument to promote their interests.

IX.
Short-sighted bias
The political time horizon is the next election. In the endeavor that the benefits of political action come quickly to their specific clienteles, the politician will favor short-term project over the long-term even if the former bring only temporary benefits and cost more in the long run than an alternative project where the costs come earlier but larger benefits later.

X.   Rational ignorance
It is rational for the individual voter in a mass democracy to remain ignorant about the political issues because the value of the individual's vote is so small that it makes not much difference for the outcome. The rational voter will vote for those candidates who promise most as benefits. Given the small relevance of an individual vote in a mass democracy, the rational voter will not spend much time and effort to investigate whether these promises are realistic or in a collision with his other desires. Thus, the political campaigns do not have information and enlightenment as the objective but disinformation and confusion. What counts, in the end, to get voted is not the solidity of the program but the enthusiasm a candidate can create with his supporters and how much he can degrade, denounce, and humiliate his opponent. The political election process spreads hatred, division, and the lust for revenge.

Antony P. Mueller

TEN FUNDAMENTAL INDICTMENTS AGAINST THE STATE

The great illusion of the modern time is the belief that a society and the economy would require a State. The State is not a necessary evil but a superfluous evil. That the individual cannot survive without a society and an economy does not mean he could not survive without a State. Anarcho-capitalism and anarcho-individualism are not against the society. The individual is not anti-social when he is anti-state. Not the anarchist is anti-social, but the State.

I

While pretending to protect life, liberty, property, the State has been the supreme enemy of life, liberty, and property. Throughout history, the crimes committed by the State have been boundlessly more than those committed by individuals.

II.

The State is not productive. The origin of the State is parasitism. The social rift is not between the worker and the capitalist but between the parasitic State and those who produce the goods.

III.

The State is the enemy of the prosperity of the people. The State confiscates wealth and punishes productivity. The State misdirects savings and investment.

IV.

Looting is the alimony of the State. The State lets the economy thrive only insofar that it provides the material for the State to plunder.

V.

Aggression is the nature of the State. Its aggression goes likewise against its own subjects as to real or imagined foreign enemies. War is the health of State.

VI.

The State creates its own enemies and thereby justifies its owns existence. Through permanent war and conflict, the State gains the consent of its underlings.

VII.

The State deceives about the legitimacy of its exercise of force and coercion. The State has no authority other than the false authority that comes through violence.

VIII.

The individual is the natural enemy of the State. Therefore, the State will do all it can to annihilate the individual and promote conformism.

IX.

All States fail. The greatest victory of the State carries with it the seed of the decay of the State.

X.

Doing away with the State will open the gate to peace and prosperity. The demise of the State marks the beginning of the triumph of the individual.

Antony P. Mueller

PRINCIPLES
OF
ECONOMIC GOVERNANCE

1. Production precedes consumption

Before something can be consumed, it must first exist. Consumption goods do not just fall from the sky. They are at the end of a long chain of intertwined production processes. To have more goods for consumption, one must first see that more goods will be produced.

2. Consumption is the final goal of production

Consumption is the objective of all economic activity, and production is its means. Current consumption results from the production process that extends to the past, yet the value of this production structure depends on the current state of valuation by the consumers and the expected future state. Therefore, the consumers are the final de facto owners of the production apparatus in a capitalist economy.

3. Production has costs

Behind every welfare check and behind each research grant lies the tax money of real people. While the taxpayers see that government confiscates part of one's personal income, they do not know to whom this money goes; and while the recipients of government expenditures see the government handing the money to them, they do not know from whom the government has taken away this money. When someone apparently gets something 'for free' from the state to consume, someone else is left with less from what he produced.

4. Value is subjective

Valuation is subjective and varies with the concrete situation and circumstances of an individual. The same physical good has different values to different persons at different times. Utility is subjective, individual, and situational. The value of a good depends on the marginal unit, not on the average or the total. There is no such thing as collective consumption. Even the temperature in the same room feels differently to different persons. The same movie or football match has a different subjective value for each viewer.

5. Productivity determines the wage rate

In a free economy, the marginal output determines the worker's wage rate. In a free labor market, businesses will hire additional workers as long as their marginal productivity exceeds and finally matches the wage rate. Competition among the firms will drive up the wage rate to the point where it is equal to productivity. The power of labor unions may change the distribution of wages among the different labor groups, but trade unions cannot change the overall wage level, which depends on labor productivity.

6. Expenditure is income and costs

Expenditure is income for the seller but represents costs for the buyer. In macroeconomic terms, spending equals income, and income equals costs. When a government spends it not only creates income but also costs. Grave policy errors are the result when government policies count only the income effect of public expenditures but ignore the cost effect.

7. Money per se is not wealth

The value of money consists in its purchasing power. Money serves as an instrument of exchange. The wealth of a person exists in its access to the goods and services he desires. An economy cannot increase its wealth by simply increasing its stock of money.

8. Labor does not create value

Labor, in combination with the other factors of production, creates products, but the value of the product depends on its utility. Utility depends on the subjective individual valuation. Employment for sake of employment makes no economic sense. What counts is value creation. To be useful, a product must offer benefits for the consumer. The value of a good exists independent from the effort of producing it.

9. Profit is the entrepreneurial reward

In competitive capitalism, economic profit is the extra bonus that those businesses earn that amend allocative errors and that best foresee the future wants of their customers. In a static economy with no change, there would be neither profit nor loss. Economic growth, however, means change, and anticipating changes is the source of economic profits.

10. Economic laws do exist

Economic laws are logical laws. As such they are invulnerable. Legal laws that contradict the fundamental economic laws do not abolish the economic laws but pervert their function. These logical economic laws work like facts. Government can ignore and try to violate the economic laws, but the economic laws will not ignore the ignorant. Those societies fare best where people and government recognize and respect these fundamental economic laws and use them to their advantage.

Antony P. Mueller

PRINCIPLES
OF
ANARCHO-CAPITALISM

I.
Each man is unique in his personality
(Human uniqueness makes the individual)

II.
Man is an enterprising being
(Human action)

III.
Society is the free association of men
(principle of the division of labor)

IV.
The limit of one person's egoism is the other person's egoism
(checks and balances)

V.
The law of cooperation is reciprocity
(*Do Ut Des*)

VI.
Government exists through consent, not by right
(Government as business management)

VII.
The source of legitimacy is the compatibility of wills
(Freedom)

VIII.
The purpose of private property is free enterprise
(Productive competition)

IX.
There are no rights and no duties other than individual self-preservation
(Scope of existence)

X.
Individual sovereignty is supreme
(Anchor)

Principles of Anarchist Individualism

I.
All I am is my property

II.
Society may limit my freedom but must not curtail my uniqueness

III.
It is better to rely on the egoism of the others than on their compassion

IV.
Society is fate - community is a choice

V.
To use oneself does not mean to be useful

VI.
To amuse oneself is an artform

VII.
I have no duty to anybody and nobody has a duty to me

VIII.
Taking people as they are, is the first step to inner and external peace

IX.
To rule over one's thoughts is the greatest achievement

X.
Not every concept represents an existence

XI.
I am my own truth

XII.
I am the measure of all things

XIII.
The principle of life - any life - is exhaustion

XIV.
My uniqueness is my perfection

XV.
A man of virtue is non-aggressive, self-controlled, superior, cheerful, ironic, open-minded, and benevolent

BIBLIOGRAPHICAL REFERENCES

Achen, Christopher H. and Larry M. Bartels: Democracy for Realists: Why Elections Do Not Produce Responsive Government (Princeton Studies in Political Behavior) Princeton University Press 2017

Antonopoulos, Andreas M.: The Internet of Money. Merkle Bloom LLC. 2016

Applebaum, Anne: Gulag. A History. Anchor Books. 2004

Applebaum, Anne: Red Famine: Stalin's War on the Ukraine. Doubleday. 2017

Ashford, Nigel and Stephen Davis (eds.): A Dictionary of Conservative and Libertarian Thought (Routledge Revivals). Routledge. 2012

Bagus, Philipp: In Defense of Deflation (Financial and Monetary Policy Studies). Springer 2014

Bagus, Phillipp and Andreas Marquart: Blind Robbery!: How the Fed, Banks and Government Steal Our Money. FinanzBuch Verlag. 2016

Baldwin, Richard: The Great Convergence: Information Technology and the New Globalization. Belknap Press. 2016

Banerjee, Abhijit, and Esther Duflo: Poor Economics: A Radical Rethinking of the Way to Fight Global Poverty. Public Affairs. 2012

Barnett, Anthony: The Athenian Option: Radical Reform for the House of Lords (Sortition and Public Policy Book 5). Imprint Academic. 2017

Barrat, James: Our Final Invention: Artificial Intelligence and the End of the Human Era. St Martin's Griffin. 2015

Belke, Ansgar and Thorsten Polleit: Monetary Economics in Globalised Financial Markets. Springer. 2009

Belloc, Hilaire: The Servile State. T. N. Foulis 1912

Benda, Julien: The Treason of the Intellectuals. Routledge. 2006

Benson, Bruce L: The Enterprise of Law: Justice Without the State. Independent Institute. 2011

Birner, Jack and Pierre Garrouste (eds): Markets, Information and Communication: Austrian Perspectives on the Internet Economy (Routledge Foundations of the Market Economy). Routledge. 2003

Block, Walter: Defending the Undefendable. Ludwig von Mises Institute. 2008

Block, Walter: The Privatization of Roads and Highways: Human and Economic Factors. CreateSpace Independent Publishing Platform. 2012

Block, Walter: Toward a Libertarian Society. Ludwig von Mises Institute. 2014

Boaz, David (ed.). The Libertarian Reader: Classic & Contemporary Writings from Lao-Tzu to Milton Friedman. Simon & Schuster 2015

Boaz, David: The Libertarian Mind. A Manifesto for Freedom. Simon & Schuster. 2015

Boehm-Bawerk, Eugen von: Karl Marx and the Close of His System: A Criticism (Classic Reprint). Forgotten Books. 2012

Boehm-Bawerk, Eugen von: Positive Theory of Capital. Ludwig von Mises Institute. 2007

Bostroum, Nick: Superintelligence: Paths, Dangers, Strategies. Oxford University Press 2016

Boetie, Etienne de la: The Politics of Obedience: The Discourse of Voluntary Servitude. With an Introduction by Murray Rothbard. Ludwig von Mises Insitute. 2015

Boettke, Peter J.: Living Economics: Yesterday, Today, and Tomorrow (Independent Studies in Political Economy). Independent Institute. 2012

Boettke, Peter J.: Calculation and Coordination: Essays on Socialism and Transitional Political Economy (Routledge Foundations of the Market Economy). Routledge 2001

Boettke, Peter J.: The Oxford Handbook of Austrian Economics (Oxford Handbooks). Oxford University Press. 2015

Boettke, Peter J.: The Political Economy of Soviet Socialism: the Formative Years, 1918-1928. 1990th Edition. Springer 1990

Boldrin, Michele and David K. Levine. Against Intellectual Monopoly. Cambridge University Press. 2010

Bourdieu, Pierre: On the State: Lectures at the College de France, 1989 - 1992. Polity 2015

Bouricius, Terry: (S)election: Sortition, the democratic alternative (Fomite Interrogations: A Series of Tracts for Our Time) (Volume 6). Fomite Publishers 2017

Boyes, William J.: Managerial Economics: Markets and the Firm (Upper Level Economics Titles). South-Western College Publications. 2011

Brafman, Ori and Rod A. Becksstrom: The Starfish and the Spider: The Unstoppable Power of Leaderless Organizations. Portfolio. 2008

Brafman, Ori and Rod A. Becksstrom: The Starfish and the Spider: The Unstoppable Power of Leaderless Organizations. Portfolio. 2008

Brackins, Daniel Alexander: Private Property, the Law, and the State. CreateSpace Independent Publishing Platform. 2017

Braun, Eduard: Finance behind the Veil of Money. CreateSpace Independent Publishing Platform. 2016

Brennan, Jason: Against Democracy. Princeton University Press. 2016

Brick, Howard: Transcending Capitalism: Visions of a New Society in Modern American Thought. Cornell University Press. 2016

Brynjolfsson, Eric and Andrew McAfee: The Second Machine Age: Work, Progress, and Prosperity in a Time of Brilliant Technologies. W. W. Norton & Company. 2016

Buchanan, James and Richard Wagner: Democracy in Deficit. The Legacy of Lord Keynes. Emerald Group Publishing. 1977

Burnheim, John: The Demarchy Manifesto. For Better Public Policy (Societas). Imprint Academic 2016

Burnheim, John: Is Democracy Possible? The Alternative to Electoral Politics. University of California Press. 1985

Burnheim, John: The Demarchy Manifesto: For Better Public Policy (Societas). Imprint Academic. 2016

Bylund, Per L.: The Problem of Production: A new theory of the firm. Routledge 2015

Cachanosky, Nicolas: Monetary Equilibrium and Nominal Income Targeting (Routledge International Studies in Money and Banking). Routledge. 2018

Caplan, Bryan: The Case against Education: Why the Education System Is a Waste of Time and Money. Princeton University Press. 2018

Caplan, Bryan: The Myth of the Rational Voter: Why Democracies Choose Bad Policies. Princeton University Press. 2008

Chafuen, Alejandro A.: Faith and Liberty: The Economic Thought of the Late Scholastics (Studies in Ethics and Economics). Lexington Books. 2003

Christinsen, Clayton M.: The Innovator's Dilemma: When New Technologies Cause Great Firms to Fail (Management of Innovation and Change). Harvard Business Review Press. 2016

Clark, Gregory: A Farewell to Alms: A Brief Economic History of the World (The Princeton Economic History of the Western World). Princeton University Press. 2009

Cogan, John F.: The High Cost of Good Intentions: A History of U.S. Federal Entitlement Programs. Princeton University Press. 2017

Conquest, Robert: The Great Terror: A Reassessment 40th anniversary Edition. Oxford University Press. 2007

Conquest, Robert: The Harvest of Sorrow: Soviet Collectivization and the Terror-Famine. Oxford University Press; Reprint edition. 1987

Cowen, Tyler and Alex Tabarrok: Modern Principles of Economics. Worth Publishers. 2014

Cowen, Tyler: Average Is Over: Powering America Beyond the Age of the Great Stagnation. Plume. 2014

Cowen, Tyler: The Great Stagnation: How America Ate All the Low-Hanging Fruit of Modern History, Got Sick, and Will (Eventually) Feel Better. Dutton 2011

Coyne, Christopher J. and Abigail R. Hall: Tyranny Comes Home: The Domestic Fate of U.S. Militarism. Stanford University Press. 2018

Cwick, Paul F.: An Investigation of Inverted Yield Curves and Economic Downturns. Ludwig von Mises Institute.

Dahlen, Michael: Ending Big Government: The Essential Case for Capitalism and Freedom. Mill City Press. 2016

Dalrymple, Theodore: Nothing but Wickedness: The Origins of the Decline of Our Culture. Gibson Square Books. 2018

Davidson, James Dale and William Rees-Mogg: The Sovereign Individual: Mastering the Transition to the Information Age. Touchstone. 1999

Delannoi, Gil and Oliver Dowlen (eds.): Sortition: Theory and Practice (Sortition and Public Policy). Imprint Academic. 2010

Deneen, Patrick J.: Why Liberalism Failed (Politics and Culture). Yale University Press. 2018

Diamandis, Peter H. and Steven Kotler: Abundance: The Future Is Better Than You Think. Free Press. Reprint edition. 2014

Di Iorio, Francesco: Cognitive Autonomy and Methodological Individualism: The Interpretative Foundations of Social Life (Studies in Applied Philosophy, Epistemology and Rational Ethics). Springer 2015

Dilorenzo Thomas J.: How Capitalism Saved America: The Untold History of Our Country, from the Pilgrims to the Present. Crown Forum. 2005

Dilorenzo, Thomas: The Problem with Socialism. Regnery Publishing. 2016

Doherty, Brian: Radicals for Capitalism: A Freewheeling History of the Modern American Libertarian Movement. Public Affairs. 2008

Dorn, James A. (ed.): Monetary Alternatives: Rethinking Government Fiat Money. Cato Institute 2017

Dorn, James A., Steve H. Hanke and Alan A. Sir Walters (eds.); The Revolution in Development Economics. Cato Institute. 1998

Dowlen, Oliver: The Political Potential of Sortition: A study of the random selection of citizens for public office (Sortition and Public Policy). Imprint Academic 2009

Drochon, Hugo: Nietzsche's Great Politics. Princeton University Press. 2016

Drucker, Peter: Innovation and Entrepreneurship. HarperBusiness. 2006

Easterbrook, Gregg: It's Better Than It Looks: Reasons for Optimism in an Age of Fear. PublicAffairs. 2018

Easterly, William R.: The Elusive Quest for Growth: Economists' Adventures and Misadventures in the Tropics. The MIT Press. 2002

Easterly, William: The White Man's Burden: Why the West's Efforts to Aid the Rest Have Done So Much Ill and So Little Good. Penguin. 2007

Easterly, William R.: The Tyranny of Experts: Economists, Dictators, and the Forgotten Rights of the Poor. Basic Books. 2015

Ebeling, Richard and Jacob G. Hornberger: The Failure of America's Foreign Wars. Future of Freedom Foundation. 1996

Ebeling, Richard M.: Monetary Central Planning and the State. The Future of Freedom Foundation. 2015

Emerson, Ralph Waldo: The Essential Writings of Ralph Waldo Emerson (Modern Library Classics). Modern Library. 2000

Eire, N. N. Carlos: Reformations: The Early Modern World, 1450-1650. Yale University Press. 2016

Eucken, Walter: The Foundations of Economics: History and Theory in the Analysis of Economic Reality. Springer. 2011

Eusepi, Guiseppe and Richard E. Wagner: Public Debt: An Illusion of Democratic Political Economy (New Thinking in Political Economy series). Edward Elgar Publications. 2017

Erhard, Ludwig: Prosperity Through Competition. Praeger. 1958

Ertel, Wolfgang: Introduction to Artificial Intelligence (Undergraduate Topics in Computer Science). Springer 2018

Evans, Anthony J.: Markets for Managers: A Managerial Economics Primer (The Wiley Finance Series). Wiley. 2014

Evans, Michelle and Augusto Zimmermann(eds.): Global Perspectives on Subsidiarity (Ius Gentium: Comparative Perspectives on Law and Justice). Springer 2014

Evans, Stanton M.: Stalin's Secret Agents: The Subversion of Roosevelt's Government. Threshold Editions. 2013

Ebeling, Richard: Austrian Economics and Public Policy. Restoring Freedom and Prosperity. The Future of Freedom Foundation. 2016

Ferguson, Niall: The Square and the Tower: Networks and Power, from the Freemasons to Facebook. Penguin Press. 2018

Ferguson, Niall: Civilization: The West and the Rest. Penguin Books. 2012

Fareed, Zakaria: The Future of Freedom: Illiberal Democracy at Home and Abroad (Revised Edition). W. W. Norton & Company. 2007

Feyerabend, Paul: Against Method. Verso. 2010

Folsom, Burton W.: The Myth of the Robber Barons: A New Look at the Rise of Big Business in America. Young America Foundation. 1991

Ford, Martin: The Rise of the Robots: Technology and the Threat of a Jobless Future. Basic Book. Reprint edition. 2015

Foss, Nikolai J. and Peter Klein (eds.): Entrepreneurship and the Firm: Austrian Perspectives on Economic Organization. Edward Elgar Publishing. 2002

Frank, Malcolm, Paul Roehrig, Ben Pring: What To Do When Machines Do Everything: How to Get Ahead in a World of AI, Algorithms, Bots, and Big Data. Wiley 2017

Friedman, David D.: The Machinery of Freedom: Guide to Radical Capitalism. CreateSpace Independent Publishing Platform; 3rd edition. 2015

Friedman, Milton and Anna Jacobson Schwartz: A Monetary History of the United States, 1867-1960. Princeton University Press. 1971

Friedman, Milton: Capitalism and Freedom. Fortieth Anniversary Edition. University of Chicago Press. 2002

Fukuyama, Francis: The Origins of Political Order: From Prehuman Times to the French Revolution. Farrar, Straus and Giroux. 2012

Garrison, Roger: Time and Money: The Macroeconomics of Capital Structure (Routledge Foundations of the Market Economy) New Edition. Routledge 2007

Gatto, John Taylor: The Underground History of American Education, Volume I: An Intimate Investigation Into the Prison of Modern Schooling. Valor Academy 2017

Guerin, Daniel (ed.): No Gods No Masters: An Anthology of Anarchism. AK Press 2005

Giddens, Anthony: The Third Way: The Renewal of Social Democracy. Polity Press. 1999

Giddens, Anthony: Capitalism and Modern Social Theory: An Analysis of the Writings of Marx, Durkheim and Max Weber. Cambridge University Press. 1973

Goodwin, Barbara: Justice by Lottery (Sortition and Public Policy). Imprint Academic 2005

Gordon, Robert J. : The Rise and Fall of American Growth: The U.S. Standard of Living since the Civil War (The Princeton Economic History of the Western World). Princeton University Press 2017

Gordon, David: An Austro-Libertarian View: Current Affairs, Foreign Policy, American History, European History (Essays by David Gordon). 3 vols. The Ludwig von Mises Institute. 2017

Granovetter, Marc: Society and Economy: Framework and Principles. Belknap Press: An Imprint of Harvard University Press. 2017

Grant, James: The Forgotten Depression: 1921: The Crash That Cured Itself. Simon & Schuster. 2014

Halberstam, Davin: The Best and the Brightest. Modern Library. 2002

Harford, Tim: Fifty Inventions that Shaped the Modern Economy. Riverhead Books. 2017

Harris, Fred and Alan Curtis (eds.): Healing Our Divided Society: Investing in America Fifty Years after the Kerner Report. Temple University Press. 2018

Haskel, Jonathan and Stian Westlake: Capitalism without Capital: The Rise of the Intangible. Princeton University Press. 2017

Hathaway, Oona A. and Scott J. Shapiro: The Internationalists: How a Radical Plan to Outlaw War Remade the World. Simon & Schuster. 2017

Hayek, Friedrich A. von: Individualism and Economic Order. University of Chicago Press. 1996

Hayek, Friedrich A. von: The Constitution of Liberty: The Definitive Edition (The Collected Works of F. A. Hayek). University of Chicago Press. 2011

Hayek, Friedrich A. von: The Road to Serfdom: Text and Documents -The Definitive Edition (The Collected Works of F. A. Hayek, Volume 2). University of Chicago Press. 2007

Hayek, Friedrich A.: Denationalisation of Money. The Argument Refined. CreateSpace Independent Publishing Platform. 2014

Hazlitt, Henry: Economics in One Lesson: The Shortest and Surest Way to Understand Basic Economics. Crown Business. 1988

Hazlitt, Henry: The Failure of the New Economics. Martino Fine Books. 2016

Heidegger, Martin: The Question Concerning Technology, and Other Essays (Harper Perennial Modern Thought). Harper Perennial Modern Classics; Reissue edition. 2013

Hennig, Brett: The End of Politicians: Time for a Real Democracy. Unbound Digital. 2017

Herbener, Jeffrey M. : Pure Time-Preference Theory of Interest. Ludwig von Mises Institute. 2011

Heyne, Paul L., Peter J. Boettke, and David L. Prychito: The Economic Way of Thinking. Pearson Series in Economics. 2013

Hicks, Stephen, R. C.: Explaining Postmodernism: Skepticism and Socialism from Rousseau to Foucault (Expanded Edition). Ockham's Razor Publishers. 2011

Higgs, Robert: Against Leviathan: Government Power and a Free Society (Independent Studies in Political Economy). Independent Institute. 2004

Higgs, Robert: Crisis and Leviathan: Critical Episodes in the Growth of American Government, 25th Anniversary Edition (Independent Studies in Political Economy). Independent Institute; Anniversary edition. 2013

Higgs, Robert: Depression, War, and Cold War: Studies in Political Economy. Oxford University Press. 2006

Higgs, Robert: Taking a Stand: Reflections on Life, Liberty, and the Economy. Independent Institute. 2015

Hirschman, Albert O.: The Passions and the Interests. Political Arguments before its Triumph (Princeton Classics). Princeton University. 2013

Hirschmann, Albert O.: Exit, Voice, and Loyalty: Responses to Decline in Firms, Organizations, and States. Harvard University Press 1970

Holcombe, Randall G.: Advanced Introduction to Public Choice (Elgar Advanced Introductions series). Edward Elgar Publishers. 2016

Holcombe, Randall G.: Advanced Introduction to the Austrian School of Economics (Elgar Advanced Introductions series). Edgar Elgar Publishers. 2014

Holcombe, Randall G.: Producing Prosperity: An Inquiry into the Operation of the Market Process (Routledge Foundations of the Market Economy). Routledge 2015

Holcombe, Randall G.: Entrepreneurship and Economic Progress (Routledge Foundations of the Market Economy). Routledge 2006

Hoppe, Hans-Hermann: A Short History of Man: Progress and Decline. Ludwig von Mises Institute 2015

Hoppe, Hans-Hermann: A Theory of Socialism and Capitalism. Ludwig von Mises Institute. 2003

Hoppe, Hans-Hermann: Democracy. The God that Failed: Economics and Politics of Monarchy, Democracy and Natural Order (Perspectives on Democratic Practice. Routledge. 2001

Hoppe, Hans-Hermann: The Economics and Ethics of Private Property: Studies in Political Economy and Philosophy, 2nd Edition. Ludwig von Mises Institute. 2010

Hoppe, Hans-Herman: The Myth of National Defense: Essays on the Theory and History of Security Production. Ludwig von Mises Institute. 2003

Horwitz, Steve: Hayek's Modern Family: Classical Liberalism and the Evolution of Social Institutions. Palgrave Macmillan. 2015

Howden, David and Joseph T. Salerno (eds.): The Fed at One Hundred: A Critical View on the Federal Reserve System. Springer. 2014

Huebert, Jacob H.: Libertarianism Today. Praeger 2010

Huerta de Soto, Jesus: Money, Bank Credit, and Economic Cycles. Ludwig von Mises Institute. 2012

Hülsmann, Jörg Guido and Stephan Kinsella (eds.): Property, Freedom, and Society: Essays in Honor of Hans-Hermann Hoppe (LvMI). Ludwig von Mises Institute 2011

Hülsmann, Jörg Guido: The Ethics of Money Production. Ludwig von Mises Institute. 2008

Humboldt, Wilhelm von: The Sphere and Duties of Government (The Limits of State Action). Martino Fine Books. 2014

Illich, Ivan: Deschooling Society (Open Forum S). Marion Boyars Publishers Ltd; New edition edition. 2000

Illich, Ivan: Limits to Medicine: Medical Nemesis, the Expropriation of Health. Marion Boyars Publishers Ltd; Revised ed. Edition. 2000

Infantino, Lorenzo: Individualism in Modern Thought: From Adam Smith to Hayek (Routledge Studies in Social and Political Thought). Routledge 2014

Irwin, Douglas A.: Against the Tide. An Intellectual History of Free Trade. Princeton University Press. 1996

Joshi, Vijay: India's Long Road: The Search for Prosperity. Oxford University Press. 2017

Juma, Calestous: Innovation and Its Enemies: Why People Resist New Technologies. Oxford University Press. 2016

Kant, Imanuel and H.S. Reiss (ed). Kant: Political Writings (Cambridge Texts in the History of Political Thought). Cambridge University Press. 1991

Kealey, Terence: The Case Against Public Science. Cato Unbound. August 2013

Kealey, Terence: The Economic Laws of Scientific Research. Palgrave Macmillan. 1996

Kengor, Paul: The Politically Incorrect Guide to Communism (The Politically Incorrect Guides). Regnery Publishing 2017

Kenny, Charles: Getting Better: Why Global Development Is Succeeding - And How We Can Improve the World Even More. Basic Books. 2012

Keynes, John Maynard: The General Theory of Employment, Interest and Money: With the Economic Consequences of the Peace (Classics of World Literature). Wordworth Editions 2017

Kinsella, Stephan: Against Intellectual Property. Ludwig von Mises Institute. 2015

Kirzner, Israel: Competition and Entrepreneurship (The Collected Works of Israel M. Kirzner). Liberty Fund. 2013

Knight, Frank: Risk, Uncertainty and Profit. Martino Fine Books. 2014

Kocka, Jürgen: Capitalism. A Short History. Princeton University Press. 2017

Kroeber, Arthur A.: China's Economy: What Everyone Needs to Know. Oxford University Press. 2016

Kuehnelt-Leddihn: Eric Ritter von: Liberty or Equality: The Challenge of Our Times. The Ludwig von Mises Institute. 2014

Kuehnelt-Leddihn: Eric Ritter von: Menace of the Herd or Procrustes at Large. Ludwig von Mises Institute. 2012

Kurer, Oskar: John Stuart Mill (Routledge Revivals): The Politics of Progress. Routledge 2018

Kurer, Oskar: The Political Foundations of Development Policies. UPA Publishers 1996

Kurlansky, Mark: Nonviolence: The History of a Dangerous Idea (Modern Library Chronicles). Modern Library 2008

Kurzweil, Ray: The Singularity Is Near: When Humans Transcend Biology. Penguin Books. 2006

Lavoie, Don: Rivalry and Central Planning. The Socialist Calculation Debate Reconsidered (Advanced Studies in Political Economy). Mercatus Center at George Mason University. 2015

Leeson, Peter: Anarchy Unbound: Why Self-Governance Works Better Than You Think (Cambridge Studies in Economics, Choice, and Society). Cambridge University Press. 2014

Leonard, Thomas C.: Illiberal Reformers: Race, Eugenics, and American Economics in the Progressive Era. Princeton University Press. 2017

Legutko, Ryszard: The Demon in Democracy: Totalitarian Temptations in Free Societies. Encounter Books. 2016

Lenin, Vladimir Ilich: State and Revolution. Martino Fine Books. 2011

Leoni, Bruno: Freedom and the Law. Liberty Fund. 1991

Lerch, Hubert: An Introduction to Political Philosophy. CreateSpace Independent Publishing Platform. 2011

Levin, Mark R.: Rediscovering Americanism: And the Tyranny of Progressivism. Threshold Editions. 2017

Levitsky, Steven and Daniel Zieblatt: How Democracies Die. Crown 2018

Lewis, Hunter: Economics in Three Lessons and One Hundred Economics Laws: Two Works in One Volume. Axios Press. 2017

Lewis, Hunter: Where Keynes Went Wrong: And Why World Governments Keep Creating Inflation, Bubbles, and Busts. Axios Press. 2009

Lilla, Mark: The Once and Future Liberal: After Identity Politics. Harper. 2017

Lindsay, Brink: The Age of Abundance: How Prosperity Transformed America's Politics and Culture. Harper Business Reprint edition. 2008

Lingle, Christopher: The Rise and Decline of the Asian Century: False Starts on the Path to the Global Millennium. Bookworld Services. 1998

Lingle, Christopher: The Rise and Decline of the Asian Century: False Starts on the Path to the Global Millennium. Bookworld Services. 1998

Machaj, Mateusz: Money, Interest, and the Structure of Production: Resolving Some Puzzles in the Theory of Capital (Capitalist Thought: Studies in Philosophy, Politics, and Economics). Lexington Books. 2017

Mallaby, Sebastian: The Man Who Knew: The Life and Times of Alan Greenspan. Penguin Books. 2017

Maltsev, Yuri: Requiem for Marx. CreateSpace Independent Publishing Platform. 1993

Maltsev, Yuri: Mass Murder and Public Slavery: The Soviet Experience. The Independent Review 2017

Mandeville, Bernard: The Fable of the Bees and Other Writings (Hackett Classics). Hacket Publishing Company. 1997

Marx, Karl: Das Kapital: A Critique of Political Economy. CreateSpace Independent Publishing Platform. 2011

Marx, Karl and Friedrich Engels: The Communist Manifesto. International Publishers Co; New edition. 2014

McCaffrey, Matthew: The Economic Theory of Costs: Foundations and New Directions (Routledge Frontiers of Political Economy). Routledge 2017

McCloskey, Deirdre: The Bourgeois Virtues: Ethics for an Age of Commerce. University of Chicago Press. 2007

McGroarty, Emmett, Jane Robbins, and Erin Tuttle: Deconstructing the Administrative State. Liberty Hill Publishing. 2017

McLuhan, Marshall: The Gutenberg Galaxy. University of Toronto Press, Scholarly Publishing Division. 2011

Menger, Carl: Principles of Economics. CreateSpace Independent Publishing Platform. 2007

Mencken, H. L.: Notes on Democracy. CreateSpace Independent Publishing Platform. 2013

Mesquita, Bruce Bueno de and Alistair Smith: The Dictator's Handbook: Why Bad Behavior is Almost Always Good Politics. PublicAffairs. 2012

Mierzejewski, Alfred C.: Ludwig Erhard: A Biography. University of North Carolina Press. 2014

Mill, John Stuart: On Liberty, Utilitarianism and Other Essays (Oxford World's Classics). Cambridge University Press. 2015

Miller, Tom: China's Asian Dream: Empire Building along the New Silk Road. Zed Books. 2017

Mises, Ludwig von: Human Action. The Scholar's Edition. Ludwig von Mises Institute. 2010

Mises, Ludwig von: Liberalism. Liberty Fund. 2005

Mises, Ludwig von: Economic Calculation in the Socialist Commonwealth. Ludwig von Mises Institute. 2012

Mises, Ludwig von: Interventionism: An Economic Analysis (Lib Works Ludwig Von Mises PB). Liberty Fund. 2011

Mokyr, Joel: A Culture of Growth: The Origins of the Modern Economy (Graz Schumpeter Lectures). Princeton University Press 2016

Mokyr, Joel: Gift of Athena: Historical Origins of the Knowledge Economy. Princeton University Press 2014

Mokyr, Joel: The Lever of Riches: Technological Creativity and Economic Progress. Oxford University Press. 1992

Molyneux, Stefan: Practical Anarchy. The Freedom of the Future. CreateSpace Independent Publishing Platform. 2017

Mueller, Antony P.: Bubble or New Era? Monetary Aspects of the New Economy. In: Birner, Jack and Pierre Garrouste (eds): Markets, Information and Communication: Austrian Perspectives on the Internet Economy (Routledge Foundations of the Market Economy). Routledge. 2003, pp. 249-261

Muller, Jerry Z.: The Tyranny of Metrics. Princeton University Press. 2018

Muller, Jerry Z.: The Mind and the Market: Capitalism in Western Thought. Anchor. 2003

Murphy, Robert: The Politically Incorrect Guide to the Great Depression and the New Deal (The Politically Incorrect Guides). Regnery Publishing. 2009

Murphy, Robert: Choice: Cooperation, Enterprise, and Human Action. Independent Institute. 2015

Molinari, Gustave de: The Production of Security. Edited by Richard Ebeling with an Introduction by Murray Rothbard. Create Space. 2009

Murray, Charles: In Our Hands: A Plan to Replace the Welfare State. AEI Press. 2016

Murray, Charles: By the People: Rebuilding Liberty Without Permission. Crown Forum. 2015

Murray, Charles: Losing Ground: American Social Policy, 1950-1980. Basic Books. 2015

Nietzsche, Friedrich: The Will to Power. Independently published. 2017

Niskanen, William A.: Reaganomics: An Insider's Account of the Policies and the People. Oxford University Press. 1988

Norberg, Johan: Ten Reasons to Look Forward to the Future. Oneworld Publication. 2017

North, Douglas C. and Robert Paul Thomas: The Rise of the Western World: A New Economic History. Cambridge University Press. 1976

North, Douglass C.: Institutions, Institutional Change and Economic Performance (Political Economy of Institutions and Decisions) Cambridge University Press. 1990

North, Gary: Mises on Money. Ludwig von Mises Institute. 2012

Novak, Michael and Paul Adams: Social Justice Isn't What You Think It Is. Encounter Books. 2015

Nozick, Robert: Anarchy, State, and Utopia. Basic Books Reprint. 2013

O'Driscoll, Gerald P. and Maria Rizzo: The Economics of Time and Ignorance. Routledge Foundations of the Market Economy. Routledge 1996

OECD (Organization for Economic Cooperation and Development: The Sources of Economic Growth in OECD Countries. OECD 2003

Oliver, Michael J.: The New Libertarianism: Anarcho-Capitalism. CreateSpace. 2013

Olson, Mancur: The Logic of Collective Action. Public Goods and the Theory of Groups. Second printing with new preface and appendix (Harvard Economic Studies). Harvard University Press. 1971

Oppenheimer, Franz: The State: Its History and Development Viewed Sociologically. (Classic Reprint). Forgotten Books. 2012

O'Rourke, P. J.: Parliament of Whores: A Lone Humorist Attempts to Explain the Entire U.S. Government. Grove Press. 2003

O'Rourke, P. J.: Eat the Rich: A Treatise on Economics. Atlantic Monthly Press. 1999

Ortega y Gasset, José: The Revolt of the Masses. W. W. Norten & Company. 1994

Ostrom, Elinor: Governing the Commons: The Evolution of Institutions for Collective Action (Canto Classics). Cambridge University Press; Reissue edition. 2015

Ostrowski, James: Progressivism: A Primer on the Idea Destroying America. Cazenovia Books. 2014

Palmer, Tom: Realizing Freedom: Libertarian Theory, History, and Practice. Cato Institute. 2014

Palmer, Tom G, Virginia Prostel, Brink Lindsey, and Tyler Cowen: Libertarianism. Past and Prospects (Cato Unbound Book 32007). Cato Institute. 2007

Parijs, Philippe Van and Yannick Vanderborght: Basic Income: A Radical Proposal for a Free Society and a Sane Economy. Harvard University Press. 2017

Paul, Ron: End the Fed. Grand Central Publishing. 2010

Paul, Ron: Revolution. A Manifesto. Grand Central Publishing. 2009

Pesek, William: Japanization: What the World Can Learn from Japan's Lost Decades. Wiley 2014

Phelps, Edmund: Mass Flourishing. How Grassroots Innovation Creates Jobs, Challenge, and Change. Princeton University Press. 2015

Pilling, David: The Growth Delusion: Wealth, Poverty, and the Well-Being of Nations. Tim Duggan Books. 2018

Pinker, Steven: Enlightenment Now: The Case for Reason, Science, Humanism, and Progress. Viking 2018

Pinker, Steven: The Better Angels of Our Nature: Why Violence Has Declined. Penguin Books. 2012

Postrel, Virginia: The Future and Its Enemies: The Growing Conflict Over Creativity, Enterprise. Free Press. 2011

Powell, Benjamin: Out of Poverty: Sweatshops in the Global Economy (Cambridge Studies in Economics, Choice, and Society). Cambridge University Press. 2014

Powell, Jim: FDR's Folly: How Roosevelt and His New Deal Prolonged the Great Depression. Crown Forum. 2004

Powell, James and Paul Johnson: The Triumph of Liberty: A 2,000 Year History Told Through the Lives of Freedom's Greatest Champions. Free Press. 2000

Qui, Insula: Capitalism Works. Independently published. 2018

Rachels, Chase and Christopher Chase Rachels: A Spontaneous Order: The Capitalist Case for a Stateless Society. CreateSpace Independent Publishing Platform. 2015

Raico, Ralph: Classical Liberalism and the Austrian School. CreateSpace Independent Publishing Platform. 2012

Raico, Ralph: Great Wars and Great Leaders: A Libertarian Rebuttal. Ludwig von Mises Institute. 2015

Ratner-Rosenhagen, Jennifer: American Nietzsche: A History of an Icon and His Ideas. University of Chicago Press; Reprint edition. 2012

Rawls, John: Justice as Fairness: A Restatement. Belknap Press: An Imprint of Harvard University Press. 2001

Rand, Ayn: Capitalism. The Unknown Ideal. Signet; Reissue edition. 1986

Reed, Lawrence R.: Great Myth of the Great Depression. Foundation for Economic Education. 2015

Reisman, George: Capitalism. A Treatise on Economics. TJS Books 1996

Reisman, George: The Government Against the Economy. Jameson Books. 1985

Reybrouck, David van: Against Elections. The Case for Democracy. Random House U.K. 2017

Reynolds, Morgan O.: Making America Poorer: The Cost of Labor Law. Cato Institute. 1987

Richman, Sheldon: America's Counter-Revolution: The Constitution Revisited. Grifien & Lash. 2016

Ridley, Matt: The Rational Optimist: How Prosperity Evolves. Harper Perennial. 2011

Rifkin, Jeremy: The Zero Marginal Cost Society: The Internet of Things, the Collaborative Commons, and the Eclipse of Capitalism. St. Martin's Griffin; Reprint edition. 2015

Ritenour, Shawn (ed.): The Mises Reader Unabridged. Ludwig von Mises Institute. 2016

Roberts, Paul Craig: The Tyranny of Good Intentions: How Prosecutors and Law Enforcement Are Trampling the Constitution in the Name of Justice. Crown. 2008

Rockwell, Llewellyn, H. Jr.: Against the State. An Anarcho-Capitalist Manifesto. Rockwell Communication. 2014

Rosenberg, Nathan and L. E. Birdzell: How the West Grew Rich: The Economic Transformation Of The Industrial World. Basic Books. 1987

Rosling, Hans, Anna Rosling Rönnlund, Ola Rosling: Factfulness: Ten Reasons We're Wrong About the World--and Why Things Are Better Than You Think. Flatiron Books 2018

Rothbard, Murray N.: Anatomy of the State. Bhpublishing. 2014

Rothbard, Murray N.: For a New Liberty. The Libertarian Manifesto. CreateSpace Independent Publishing Platform. 2006

Rothbard, Murray N.: What Has Government Done to Our Money? Ludwig von Mises Institute. 2015

Rothbard, Murray N.: Man, Economy, and State with Power and Market, Scholar's Edition. Ludwig von Mises Institute. 2011

Rothbard, Murray N.: America's Great Depression. Ludwig von Mises Institute. 2000

Rummel, Rudy J.: Death by Government: Genocide and Mass Murder Since 1900. Routledge 1997

Rummel, Rudy J.: The Blue Book of Freedom: Ending Famine, Poverty, Democide, and War. Cumberland House Publishing. 2007

Salerno, Joseph T.: Money: Sound and Unsound. Ludwig von Mises Institute. 2015

Say, Jean-Baptiste: A Treatise on Political Economy: Or the Production, Distribution and Consumption of Wealth. CreateSpace Independent Publishing Platform. 2013

Schiff, Peter: How an Economy Grows and Why It Crashes. Wiley. 2010

Schmitt, Carl: The Leviathan in the State Theory of Thomas Hobbes: Meaning and Failure of a Political Symbol (Heritage of Sociology). University of Chicago Press Ed Edition. 2008

Schmitt, Carl: The Concept of the Political: Expanded Edition Enlarged Edition with a Commentary by Leo Strauss. The University of Chicago Press. 2007

Schoolland, Ken: The Adventures of Jonathan Gullible. A Free Market Odyssey. Liberty Publishing. 2011

Schumpeter, Joseph A.: Business Cycles: A Theoretical, Historical, and Statistical Analysis of the Capitalist Process (2 Vols.). Martino Fine Books. 2017

Schumpeter, Joseph A.: Can Capitalism Survive?: Creative Destruction and the Future of the Global Economy. Harper Perennial Modern Classics. 2009

Schumpeter, Joseph A.: Capitalism, Socialism, and Democracy: Third Edition. Harper Perennial Modern Classics. 2008

Schumpeter, Joseph A.: Essays: On Entrepreneurs, Innovations, Business Cycles and the Evolution of Capitalism. Routledge 1989

Schumpeter, Joseph A.: Theory of Economic Development (Social Science Classics Series). Routledge 1981

Schwab, Klaus and Nicholas Davis, Satya Nadella: Shaping the Fourth Industrial Revolution. World Economic Forum. 2018

Scruton, Roger: Fools, Frauds and Firebrands: Thinkers of the New Left. Bloomsbury Continuum. 2017

Selgin, George: Financial Stability without Central Banks. London Publishing Partnership. 2018

Selgin, George: Money: Free and Unfree. Cato Institute. 2017

Selgin, George: Less Than Zero. The Case for a Falling Price Level in a Growing Economy. CreateSpace Independent Publishing Platform. 2014

Selgin, George: The Theory of Free Banking. Rowman & Littlefield Publisher. 1988

Sen, Amartya: Development as Freedom. Anchor. 2000

Sévillia, Jean: Le terrorisme intellectuel (French Edition). Tempus Perrain. 2017

Shaffer, Butler: Boundaries of Order: Private Property as a Social System. CreateSpace Independent Publishing Platform. 2009

Shaffer, Buttler: The Wizards of Ozymandias: Reflections on the Decline and Fall. CreateSpace Independent Publishing Platform. 2012

Shlae, Amity: The Forgotten Man: A New History of the Great Depression Harper Perennial. 2008

Simon, Julian Lincoln: The Ultimate Resource 2. Princeton University Press. 1998

Sintomer, Yves: Das demokratische Experiment: Geschichte des Losverfahrens in der Politik von Athen bis heute (German Edition). Springer 2016

Smiley, Gene: Rethinking the Great Depression (American Ways). Ivan R. Dee Publisher. 2003

Smith, Adam: The Theory of Moral Sentiments. Digireads.com. 2010

Smith, Adam: The Wealth of Nations (Bantam Classics). Bantam Classics; Annotated edition. 2003

Snyder, Timothy: On Tyranny: Twenty Lessons from the Twentieth Century. Tim Duggan Books. 2017

Sombart, Werner: The Quintessence Of Capitalism: A Study Of The History And Psychology Of The Modern Business Man. Scholar Select. Andesite Press. 2017

Solzhenitsyn, Aleksandr: The Gulag Archipelago. The Harvill Press. 2003

Soto, Hernando de: The Mystery of Capital: Why Capitalism Triumphs in the West and Fails Everywhere Else. Basic Books. 2003

Sowell, Thomas: Basic Economics. Basic Books. 2014

Sowell, Thomas: Economic Facts and Fallacies. Basic Books. 2011

Sowell, Thomas: The Quest for Cosmic Justice. Free Press 2002

Spencer, Herbert: Social Statics: Or, The Conditions Essential to Human Happiness Specified and the First of them Developed. Nabu Press. 2011

Srinivasa, Bhu: Americana: A 400-Year History of American Capitalism. Penguin Press. 2017

Steil, Ben: The Marshall Plan: Dawn of the Cold War. Simon & Schuster. 2018

Steil, Ben: The Battle of Bretton Woods: John Maynard Keynes, Harry Dexter White, and the Making of a New World Order (Council on Foreign Relations Books). Princeton University Press. 2014

Stirner, Max: The Ego and His Own: The Case of the Individual Against Authority (Dover Books on Western Philosophy). Dover Publications. 2005

Stone, Peter: Lotteries in Public Life: A Reader (Sortition and Public Policy). Imprint Academic. 2012

Stringham, Edward Peter: Private Governance: Creating Order in Economic and Social Life. Oxford University Press. 2015

Susskind, Richard and Daniel Susskind: The Future of the Professions: How Technology Will Transform the Work of Human Experts. Oxford University Press. Reprint edition. 2017

Suvorov, Viktor: Icebreaker. Who Started the Second World War? PL UK Publishing. 2012

Taleb, Nassim Nicholas: Skin in the Game: Hidden Asymmetries in Daily Life. Random House 2018

Taylor, Frederick: The Downfall of Money: Germany's Hyperinflation and the Destruction of the Middle Class. Bloomsbury Press. 2015

Taylor, Mark Zachary: The Politics of Innovation: Why Some Countries Are Better Than Others at Science and Technology. Oxford University Press. 2016

Thiel, Peter: Zero to One: Notes on Startups, or How to Build the Future. Currency Publishers. 2014

Thornton, Mark: The Bastiat Collection. Ludwig von Mises Institute. 2017

Thornton, Mark: The Economics of Prohibition. Ludwig von Mises Institute. 2014

Tilly, Charles: Coercion, Capital and European States, A.D. 990 – 1992. Wiley-Blackwell. 1992

Tirole, Jean: Economics for the Common Good. Princeton University Press. 2017

Tooley, Hunt: The Great War: Western Front and Home Front. Palgrave 2015

Tucker, Jeffrey: A Beautiful Anarchy: How to Create Your Own Civilization in the Digital Age. Laissez Faire Books. 2012

Vance, Laurence M.: War, Empire, and the Military: Essays on the Follies of War and U.S. Foreign Policy. Vance Publications. 2014

Vedder, Richard: Going Broke By Degree: Why College Cost. AEI Press. 2004

Veryser, Harry C.: It Didn't Have to be This Way: Why Boom and Bust Is Unncessary - and How the Austrian School of Economics Breaks the Cycle (Culture of Enterprise).ISI Books.2013

Volcker, Paul and Toyoo Gyohten. Changing Fortunes. Crown. 1992

Walsh, Michael: The Devil's Pleasure Palace: The Cult of Critical Theory and the Subversion of the West. Encounter Books. 2017

White, Lawrence: The Clash of Economic Ideas: The Great Policy Debates and Experiments of the Last Hundred Years. Cambridge University Press. 2012

White, Lawrence: The Theory of Monetary Institutions. Wiley-Blackwell. 1999

White, Lawrence: Competition and Currency: Essays on Free Banking and Money. New York University Press. 1992

Wisniewski, Jakub: The Economics of Law, Order, and Action: The Logic of Public Goods (Routledge Advances in Heterodox Economics). Routledge. 2018

Williams, Walter E.: American Contempt for Liberty (Hoover Institution Press Publication). Hoover Institution Press 2015 Williams, Walter E.: Race & Economics: How Much Can Be Blamed on Discrimination?. Hoover Institution Press. 2011

Wolfram, Gary: A Capitalist Manifesto: Understanding The Market Economy And Defending Liberty. Dunlap Goddard. 2013

Woods, Thomas E.: Meltdown: A Free-Market Look at Why the Stock Market Collapsed, the Economy Tanked, and Government Bailouts Will Make Things Worse. Regnery 2009

Yergin, Daniel and Joseph Stanislaw: The Commanding Heights: The Battle for the World Economy. Free Press. 2002

Zelmanovitz, Leonidas: The Ontology and Function of Money: The Philosophical Fundamentals of Monetary Institutions (Capitalist Thought: Studies in Philosophy, Politics, and Economics). Lexington Books 2015

Appendix

Anarcho-Capitalism: An Annotated Bibliography
by Hans-Hermann Hoppe

Here is the essential reading on anarcho-capitalism, which might also be called the natural order, private-property anarchy, ordered anarchy, radical capitalism, the private-law society, or society without a state. This is not intended to be a comprehensive list. Indeed, only English-language works currently in print or forthcoming are included. Please note that suggestions are welcome, especially for Section IV: Congenial Writings.

I. Murray N. Rothbard and Austro-Libertarianism

At the top of any reading list on anarcho-capitalism must be the name Murray N. Rothbard. There would be no anarcho-capitalist movement to speak of without Rothbard. His work has inspired and defined the thinking even of such libertarians such as R. Nozick, for instance, who have significantly deviated from Rothbard, whether methodologically or substantively. Rothbard's entire work is relevant to the subject of anarcho-capitalism, but centrally important are:

The Ethics of Liberty, the most comprehensive presentation and defense of a libertarian law code yet written. Grounded in the tradition of natural law and in its style of axiomatic-deductive reasoning, Rothbard explains the concepts of human rights, self-ownership, original appropriation, contract, aggression, and punishment. He demonstrates the moral unjustifiability of the state, and offers smashing refutations of prominent limited-statist libertarians such as L. v. Mises, F. A. Hayek, I. Berlin, and R. Nozick.

In For A New Liberty Rothbard applies abstract libertarian principles to solve current welfare-state problems. How would a stateless society provide for goods such as education, money, streets, police, courts, national defense, social security, environmental protection, etc.? Here are the answers.

Power and Market is the most comprehensive theoretical analysis of the inefficiencies and counterproductive effects of every conceivable form of government interference with the market, from price controls, compulsory cartels, anti-trust laws, licenses, tariffs, child labor laws, patents, to any form of taxation (including Henry George's proposed "single tax" on ground land).

Egalitarianism As a Revolt Against Nature is a marvelous collection of Rothbard essays on philosophical, economic, and historical aspects of libertarianism, ranging from war and revolution to kids' and women's liberation. Rothbard shows his intellectual debt both to Ludwig von Mises and Austrian economics (praxeology) and to Lysander Spooner and Benjamin Tucker and individualist-anarchist political philosophy. This collection is the best single introduction to Rothbard and his libertarian research program.

The four-volume Conceived in Liberty is a comprehensive narrative history of colonial America and the role of libertarian ideas and movements. Rothbard's magisterial two-volume An Austrian Perspective on the History of Economic Thought traces the development of libertarian economic and philosophical thought throughout intellectual history. The Irrepressible Rothbard contains delightful libertarian commentary on political, social, and cultural issues, written during the last decade of Rothbard's life.

Justin Raimondo has written an insightful biography: Murray N. Rothbard: An Enemy of the State.

The Austro-libertarian tradition inaugurated by Rothbard is continued by Hans-Hermann Hoppe. In Democracy — The God That Failed Hoppe compares monarchy favorably to democracy, but criticizes both as ethically and economically inefficient, and advocates a natural order with competitive security and insurance suppliers. He revises fundamental orthodox historical interpretations, and reconsiders central questions of libertarian strategy. The Economics and Ethics of Private Property includes Hoppe's axiomatic defense of the principle of self-ownership and original appropriation: anyone arguing against these principles is involved in a performative or practical contradiction.

The Myth of National Defense is a collection of essays by an international assembly of social scientists concerning the relationship between State and war and the possibility of non-statist property defense: by militias, mercenaries, guerrillas, protection-insurance agencies, etc.

II. Alternative Approaches to Anarcho-Capitalism

The following authors come to similar conclusions but reach them in different ways and varying styles. While Rothbard and Hoppe are natural-rightsers of sorts and praxeologists, there exist also utilitarian, deontic, empiricist, historicist, positivist, and plain eclectic defenders of anarcho-capitalism.

Randy E. Barnett's The Structure of Liberty is an outstanding discussion of the requirements of a liberal-libertarian society from the viewpoint of a lawyer and legal theorist. Heavily influenced by F.A. Hayek, Barnett uses the term "polycentric constitutional order" for anarcho-capitalism.

Bruce L. Benson's The Enterprise of Law is the most comprehensive empirical-historical study of anarcho-capitalism. Benson provides abundant empirical evidence for the efficient operation of market-produced law and order. Benson's sequel To Serve and Protect is likewise to be recommended.

David D. Friedman's The Machinery of Freedom presents the utilitarian case for anarcho-capitalism: brief, easy to read, and with many applications from education to property protection.

Anthony de Jasay favors a deontic approach to ethics. His writing — in The State, in Choice, Contract, Consent, and the excellent essay collection Against Politics — is theoretical, with a neo-classical, game-theoretic flavor. Brilliant critic of public choice and constitutional economics — and the notion of minarchism.

Morris and Linda Tannehill's <u>The Market for Liberty</u> has a distinctly Randian flavor. However, the authors employ Ayn Rand's pro-state argument in support of the opposite, anarchistic conclusion. Outstanding yet much neglected analysis of the operation of competing security producers (insurers, arbitrators, etc.).

III. Precursors of Modern Anarcho-Capitalism

The contemporary anarcho-capitalist intellectual movement has a few outstanding 19th and early-20th century precursors. Even when sometimes deficient — the issue of ground land ownership in the tradition of Herbert Spencer and the theory of money and interest in the Spooner-Tucker tradition — the following titles remain indispensable and largely unsurpassed. (This listing is chronological and systematic, rather than alphabetical.)

Gustave de Molinari's pathbreaking 1849 article <u>The Production of Security</u> is probably the single most important contribution to the modern theory of anarcho-capitalism. Molinari argues that monopoly is bad for consumers, and that this also holds in the case of a monopoly of protection. Demands competition in the area of security production as for every other line of production.

Herbert Spencer's <u>Social Statics</u> is an outstanding philosophical discussion of natural rights in the tradition of John Locke. Spencer defends the right to ignore the state. Also highly recommended are his <u>Principles of Ethics</u>.

Auberon Herbert is a student of Spencer. In <u>The Right and Wrong of Compulsion by the State</u>, Herbert develops the Spencerian idea of equal freedom to its logically consistent anarcho-capitalist end. Herbert is the father of Voluntaryism.

Lysander Spooner is a 19th-century American lawyer and legal theorist. No one who has read "No Treason," included in **The Lysander Spooner Reader**, will ever see government with the same eyes. Spooner makes mincemeat of the idea of a social contract.

A concise history of individualist-anarchist thought and the related movement in 19th-century America, with particular attention to Spooner and Benjamin Tucker, is James J. Martin's <u>Men Against the State</u>.

Franz Oppenheimer is a left-anarchist German sociologist. In <u>The State</u> he distinguishes between the economic (peaceful and productive) and the political (coercive and parasitic) means of wealth acquisition, and explains the state as instrument of domination and exploitation.

Albert J. Nock is influenced by Franz Oppenheimer. In <u>Our Enemy, the State</u> he explains the anti-social, predatory nature of the state, and draws a sharp distinction between government as voluntarily acknowledged authority and the State. Nock in turn influenced Frank Chodorov, who would influence young Murray Rothbard. In his <u>Fugitive Essays</u>, a collection of pro-market, anti-state political and economic commentary, Chodorov attacks taxation as robbery.

IV. Congenial Writings

While not directly concerned with the subject of anarcho-capitalism and written by less-than-radical libertarian or even non-libertarian authors, the following are invaluable for a profound understanding of liberty, natural order, and the state.

John V. Denson's The Costs of War is a collection of essays by a distinguished group of libertarian and paleo-conservative scholars from various disciplines. Exposes the aggressive nature of the state. Possibly the most powerful anti-war book ever. Also to be recommended is Denson's collection Reassessing the Presidency on the growth of state power.

David Gordon's Secession, State, and Liberty is a collection of essays by contemporary philosophers, economists, and historians in defense of the right to secession.

Friedrich A. Hayek, Law, Legislation, and Liberty, Vol. 1, is an important study on the "spontaneous" evolution of law, and the distinction of law versus legislation and between private and public law.

Bertrand de Jouvenel, On Power, is an outstanding account of the growth of state power, with many important insights concerning the role of the aristocracy as defender of liberty and mass democracy as a promoter of state power. Related, and likewise to be recommended is his Sovereignty.

Etienne de la Botie, The Politics of Obedience, is the classic 16th-century inquiry into the source of government power. La Botie shows that the state's power rests exclusively on public "opinion." By implication, every state can be made to crumble — instantly and without any violence — simply by virtue of a change in public opinion.

Bruno Leoni, Freedom and the Law, is an earlier and in some regards superior treatment of topics similar to those discussed by Hayek. Leoni portrays Roman law as something discovered by independent judges rather than enacted or legislated by central authority — and thus akin to English common law.

Robert Nisbet, The Quest for Community (formerly published under the more descriptive title Community and Power) explains the protective function of intermediate social institutions, and the tendency of the state to weaken and destroy these institutions in order to gain total control over the isolated individual.

The Journal of Libertarian Studies. An Interdisciplinary Quarterly Review, founded by Murray N. Rothbard and now edited by Hans-Hermann Hoppe, is an indispensable resource for any serious student of anarcho-capitalism and libertarian scholarship

The following JLS articles are most directly concerned with anarcho-capitalism.

Anderson, Terry, and P.J. Hill, The American Experiment in Anarcho-Capitalism, 3, 1.

Barnett, Randy E., Whither Anarchy? Has Robert Nozick Justified the State?, 1,1.

——, Toward a Theory of Legal Naturalism, 2, 2.

Benson, Bruce L., Enforcement of Private Property Rights in Primitive Societies, 9,1.

——, Customary Law with Private Means of Resolving Disputes and Dispensing Justice, 9,2.

——, Reciprocal Exchange as the Basis for Recognition of Law, 10, 1.

——, Restitution in Theory and Practice, 12, 1.

Block, Walter, Free Market Transportation: Denationalizing the Roads, 3, 2.

——, Hayek's Road to Serfdom, 12, 2.

Childs, Roy A. Jr., The Invisible Hand Strikes Back, 1,1.

Cuzan, Alfred G., Do We Ever Really Get Out Of Anarchy?, 3, 2.

Davidson, James D., Note on Anarchy, State, and Utopia, 1, 4.

Eshelman, Larry, Might versus Right, 12, 1.

Evers, Williamson M., Toward a Reformulation of the Law of Contracts, 1, 1.

——, The Law of Omissions and Neglect of Children, 2, 1.

Ferrara, Peter J., Retribution and Restitution: A Synthesis, 6, 2.

Fielding, Karl T., The Role of Personal Justice in Anarcho-Capitalism, 2, 3.

Grinder, Walter E., and John Hagel, III, Toward a Theory of State Capitalism, 1, 1.

Hart, David M., Gustave de Molinari and the Anti-Statist Liberal Tradition, 3 parts, 5, 3 to 6, 1.

Hoppe, Hans-Hermann, Fallacies of Public Goods Theory and the Production of Security, 9, 1.

——, Marxist and Austrian Class Analysis, 9, 2.

——, The Private Production of Defense, 14, 1.

Kinsella, N. Stephan, Punishment and Proportionality, 12, 1.

——, New Rationalist Directions in Libertarian Rights Theory, 12, 2.

——, Inalienability and Punishment, 14, 1.

Liggio, Leonard P., Charles Dunoyer and French Classical Liberalism, 1, 3.

Mack, Eric, Voluntaryism: The Political Thought of Auberon Herbert, 2, 4.

McElroy, Wendy, The Culture of Individualist Anarchism in Late 19th-Century America, 5, 3.

McGee, Robert W., Secession Reconsidered, 11, 1.

Osterfeld, David, Internal Inconsistencies in Arguments for Government: Nozick, Rand, Hospers, 4, 3.

——, Anarchism and the Public Goods Issue: Law, Courts, and the Police, 9, 1.

Paul, Jeffrey, Nozick, Anarchism, and Procedural Rights, 1, 4.

Peden, Joseph R., Property Rights in Celtic Irish Law, 1, 2.

Peterson, Steven A., Moral Development and Critiques of Anarchism, 8, 2.

Raico, Ralph, Classical Liberal Exploitation Theory, 1, 3.

Rothbard, Murray N., Robert Nozick and the Immaculate Conception of the State, 1, 1.

——, Concepts of the Role of Intellectuals in Social Change Toward Laissez Faire, 9, 2.

——, Nations by Consent: Decomposing the Nation-State, 11, 1.

Sanders, John T., The Free Market Model versus Government: A Reply to Nozick, 1, 1.

Smith, George H., Justice Entrepreneurship in a Free Market, 3, 4 (with comments by Steven Strasnick, Robert Formani and Randy Barnett and a reply by Smith, in the same issue).

Sneed, John D., Order without Law: Where will Anarchists Keep the Madmen?, 1, 2.

Stringham, Edward, Market Chosen Law, 14, 1.

Tinsley, Patrick, Private Police: A Note, 14,1.

Watner, Carl, The Proprietary Theory of Justice in the Libertarian Tradition, 6, 3—4.

Source:
https://www.lewrockwell.com/2001/12/hans-hermann-hoppe/anarcho-capitalism-2/

***

Antony P. Mueller

ABOUT THE AUTHOR

German-born Antony Peter Mueller is a professor of economics currently at the federal university UFS in Brazil.
Over his academic career, Antony P. Mueller held positions and did research at universities in Europe, the United States, where he was a Fulbright scholar, and Latin America.
His publications cover macroeconomics, monetary policy, sovereign risk analysis, social and economic policy issues, and economic and monetary integration.
Antony P. Mueller is a senior fellow of the American Institute of Economic Research (AIER), an associate scholar of the Ludwig von Mises Institute, USA, and a member by merit of the Brazilian Mises Institute (IMB).
He obtained his doctorate in economics summa cum laude from the University of Erlangen-Nuremberg, Germany.

Websites:
http://www.continentaleconomics.com/
http://capitalstudies.org/
Amazon author's page
https://www.amazon.com/-/e/B07BHF4RG8
CONTACT: *antonymueller@gmx.com*